POWER GOLF

POWER GOLF

Ian Woosnam

with Bruce Critchley

Lyons & Burford, Publishers

Printed in the United States of America

10 9 8 7 6 5 4 3 2 1

Library of Congress Cataloging-in-Publication Data

Woosnam, Ian.
    Power golf / Ian Woosnam : with Bruce Critchley.
        p.   cm.
    ISBN 1-55821-196-9
    1. Swing (Golf)   I. Critchley, Bruce.   II. Title.
GV979.S9W66   1992
796.352'3—dc20   92-14388
                                                        CIP

First published in Great Britain by Stanley Paul.

Acknowledgements

For permission to reproduce copyright photographs,
the publishers would like to thank Phil Sheldon,
Lawrence Levy, Peter Dazeley, AllSport,
Matthew Harris, Bob Thomas and Michael Hobbs

Contents

Introduction

I have always held the somewhat sceptical view that the moment a great golfer reveals all about his own golf game and advises others in print what has been successful for him, that's the end of his greatness as a golfer.

Almost before he had started to make an impact and was still a gleam in his manager's eye, Bobby Clampit was endorsing the works of some golfing guru and describing the umpteen procedures he went through as a preliminary to hitting the ball. That, and a highly visible disaster at Troon in the Open Championship, may be the reason why he has never fully realized his great potential. Johnny Miller was another whose magical talent seemed to desert him the moment he tried to explain in print the secrets of his success.

I therefore approached the project of working with Ian Woosnam on a book about his golf game with not a little trepidation, fearful that what we were about to do might break the spell. However, Ian's approach to golf is so single-minded and straightforward that the side show of collaborating on a book would be unlikely to interfere with his main purpose in life – that of winning golf titles.

Ian, to be honest, has paid little attention to the written word when it comes to learning and perfecting this most exasperating of games. As he himself says, if he had tried to model his game along the lines almost universally preached when he was growing up, the world might never have heard of Ian Woosnam the golfer. The upright swing, that was for many years regarded as the only way to play the game consistently well, would have been a disaster for someone of his stature.

Whilst there is no suggestion that Nick Faldo saw Ian hit a golf ball and then decided to try and play the same way, Nick has remodelled his swing so that he now does by intention what Ian does naturally. Also, much of today's teaching is based on the rounder, flatter swing that is so much the Woosnam style. Ian would never claim that it is his success that has broken the mould of consensus opinion as to how to swing the club; it is just that he happens to be a completely natural example of what is now perceived to be the best way of hitting a golf ball.

In our early discussions, I soon realized that writing this book might not be as difficult as I feared, in that both our formative golfing years were very similar. Both of us were small for our years and spent all our time on the golf course trying to keep up with older and bigger friends and relations. We both developed swings that enabled us to achieve this and when we grew up those swings matured into vehicles for propelling the ball further than most. Although today of differing stature, our solution to that early problem of keeping up with the pack was very similar.

I should add that that was where our golf games parted company. I was persuaded that a long, wristy swing could never be made to stand up under pressure and tried to change it. Ian, being of sterner stuff, worked on with the staggering results we see today.

It is the dream of every aspiring golfer to emulate the swing of a Ballesteros, a Faldo or a Woosnam and have every drive soar away over the 280-yard mark. That is so much more attractive than the ambition to take only thirty putts a round and certainly the reason that the driving ranges around the world are full, while the practice greens are deserted.

In truth, though, swings like theirs can only evolve if the game is taken up at a fairly early age and grows as the body develops. Big men have taken the game up later in life and hit the ball great distances, but never with the same ease and grace of today's great players.

In this book, Ian explains what he believes are the mechanics behind his big hitting and offers some suggestions how greater distance can be achieved, hopefully without a catastrophic loss of accuracy. He, as much as anyone, knows that length is a two-edged sword; the further you hit the ball, the narrower the margin for error.

One of the great teachers of the post war years, Tom Haliburton, once said, 'Golf is basically a simple game, made difficult by man.' Ian has tried in this book to keep it simple and to put forward ideas and concepts that are both understandable and practical.

One of his own great strengths has been his refusal to complicate the game and never let himself get bogged down with theory. He has persevered with the swing he grew up with, and that, allied to great determination, has got him where he is today.

BRUCE CRITCHLEY

1 My Formative Years

Starting off

I cannot remember how young I was when I knew golf was going to be my life. Sport was always an important part of my childhood, Dad having been a keen footballer who turned to golf towards the end of his playing career. I was seven years old at the time and enjoyed anything to do with games. Football, with Dad's influence, was important, but so was golf which we both started at about the same time.

Having an elder brother and sister and always a bit on the short side, my main aim in the early years was to try and keep up with them. I did not find hitting a golf ball difficult, but I expect that's true of most kids who start young. From the beginning, if I had a problem, it was hitting the ball straight, but that was of secondary importance to keeping up with my brother and sister.

Throughout my life, I have always drawn the ball and I think this goes back to those early days, playing with clubs that were probably a bit big for me. Inevitably, the toe of the club was off the ground and with a flat, round swing, the only possible shape of shot was a hook. There was a quite long period when I tried to cure the draw and hit the ball with a fade, but I wasn't any more consistent and I lost a lot of length. Since then I have concentrated on making what I've got work, rather than trying to change to something unnatural.

I must have been twenty or twenty-one before I realized the importance of getting the lie of the club right. That is to say, making sure the sole of the club is flat on the ground at the address. I have always tended to stand a long way from the ball, relative to my height, and any normal club in my hands would have the toe sticking up in the air.

A year or two before that, I had borrowed a friend's Ping 1-iron and couldn't get on with it at all. Everyone else was switching to that particular make, but it wouldn't work for me. It was just that the club was too upright for me. It was five or six years before I came back to that make of 1-iron, this time the right shape for me, and I have used one ever since.

One thing my early sporting background gave me was finding out what fun it was to win. Not surprisingly, I also found I hated to lose. For that reason golf, because it was an individual game with the outcome determined by the player himself, was always going to triumph over football, the team game. I clearly remember the moment of the parting of the ways. When I was fourteen, there were a golf match and a football game on the same day. I opted for golf and that was that. I will always be grateful to football for giving me strong legs, a vital asset for a good golfer both from a stamina point of view and for hitting the ball a long way.

I never made a conscious decision about becoming a professional; I just knew that I was going to earn my living playing golf. It never entered my head that I might not be good enough to play with the best in Europe or that one day I would not be up there with them. For this reason I didn't pay much attention to an amateur career: it was more a means of enjoying competition until I was old enough to turn pro.

From the age of fifteen, I played representative golf at various levels: Shropshire Juniors and Seniors, Welsh boys and a full Welsh international in a friendly match against France when I was 18. I was later picked for the Home Internationals in September 1976, but a bout of glandular fever ruled me out of that. With the Tour qualifying school later that autumn, I wasted no time signing professional papers and was on my way.

Making a living

The early years were hard. I had no trouble getting my player's card but in those days all *that* entitled you to do was enter the pre-qualifying events. I got through to a few tournaments but could not make enough money to keep the card, so had to go back to the school in the autum of both '77 and '78.

Money was the root of the problem and it was only by doing well in local professional competitions that I earned enough to play perhaps ten Tour events each year. Certainly in those first few years, I found playing alongside the Faldos and the Ballesteroses intimidating. I knew I could put rounds together as well as they could, and it was frustrating not to be able to do it when it mattered.

After 1978, I did well enough to keep my card, but that was just about all. The Tour was still a luxury, funded by successes locally. But I felt I was

Haircuts were a luxury in the early days!

learning all the time, getting better. I was starting to put a few good rounds together, but hardly ever two in a row, let alone four. However, the odd round in the sixties told me I was capable of holding my own at this level and I was getting the occasional taste of playing alongside the best. What was more importnat, I was also losing the fear of doing so.

About this time, a local firm gave me £5000 a year in return for 50 per cent of my winnings. In the first couple of years, they got nothing back, but it enabled me to stick with the Tour and build on the experience. Suddenly, in 1982, I won my first tournament and went from 104th in the order of merit to 8th and never looked back.

I had learned two great lessons the previous year. I was on the African circuit in the early spring of 1981 and as usual playing well without really scoring. One day on the practice ground, I was next to Gordon J. Brand. He was firing the ball all over the place, while I just kept hitting them straight at the target. What impressed me was that he wasn't at all perturbed and

11

that week continually scored in or near the 60s while I was up in the high 70s. From that day onwards I stopped worrying about the occasional bad shot or hole. I adopted the philosophy that I was good enough to get five birdies a round and should still have a good score even if I dropped the odd shot here or there. That spring in Africa, I put together the first decent competitive golf of my life and finished 6th on the Safari Tour.

The second lesson came at the end of that Tour. I took three weeks off and never hit another shot that year – a mistake. Since then I've continued to play as much as possible, particularly when I'm playing well. I thrive on competition.

The next year, 1982, I again played well in Africa, and most important of all, by finishing 3rd on the Safari Tour, became exempt from the dreaded pre-qualifying events. Not long after that I finished 2nd in the Italian Open and with the £5000 I won there, removed that other barrier to progress – financial worries for the year. Of equal importance, I proved to myself there that I could perform with Europe's top players around me. That gave me the confidence to go and do it again and I had five more 2nd places that year as well as my first Tour victory in the Swiss Open.

Learning to win

Now the knowledge of how to play winning golf was coming thick and fast. I soon realized that it wasn't just me who was nervous when in contention. We all were and how ever often you've won and however much money you've made, you still get nervous over those closing holes. The only difference is you learn to handle it better. Above all you think more clearly under pressure.

Certainly the experience gained during those five 2nd places in the summer of '82 contributed greatly towards coping with the situation when presented with the chance of winning in Switzerland. I had chances before that year and although I hadn't taken them, I had learned all the time. Only a week or two before I had had a putt to beat Greg Norman in the Benson & Hedges at York and could hardly hold the putter, I was so nervous. At Crans, it was Bill Longmuir who missed the short putt in the play-off and the first victory was in the bag.

Thereafter it has been fun and rewarding, with at least one victory most years and even better performances on the European order of merit, proof of a continuing improvement. And my confidence was growing. There were still bad weeks and missed opportunities, but the knowledge that my best game

One of my first wins, the Silk Cut Masters in 1983

was capable of winning anywhere, plus the financial security of half a dozen years near the top, meant that I was able to adopt the patience necessary to make the most of the chances when they came.

My greatest year

All that was before 1987. That year, everything fell into place. An early win in Hong Kong, a great start in Europe with two quick victories and the roller coaster started, never to stop till the year end.

The significant moments mostly came outside the European Tour, though success on the Tour was the launching pad. World golf is so structured that the best players from the European, American and Far East circuits are rewarded for a good year with invitations to a number of rich, limited-field events. The longest standing of these is the World Match Play, though now there are two or three comparable events in the Far East, such as the Kirin Cup, plus the biannual World Cup, the Dunhill Cup and the Sun City event. If you can hold your game together through October and November, then good performances in just a handful of tournaments can double or treble the year's earnings.

The World Match Play was, for me, a very special tournament. Up to then I had had a great year and could justifiably claim to be the best in Europe. The World Match Play, with victories over Nick Faldo, Seve Ballesteros and Sandy Lyle on successive days, was confirmation that on my day I was as good as anyone in the world. What was especially pleasing was to hole 6-footers against both Nick and Seve on the final green. Anyone who says their knees are not knocking at moments like that has to be lying!

Later in the year, I got an enormous kick out of winning the World Cup with David Llewellyn and it tickled us pink to think that our little country could take on and beat the best in the world. It would be hard for me to say when I played my best in 1987, but the golf I played that week in Hawaii would have to be a contender.

The Sun City tournament is not the most popular event on the calendar for a number of pretty obvious reasons. However, it was important to me. First of all, that $1m first prize meant financial security for the rest of my life and that is a great feeling. Secondly, however the media may speculate, you are playing for $1m, winner-take-all. I don't care who you are, the 'duck or no dinner' situation of that tournament really gets the adrenalin flowing. Nick Faldo and I were neck-and-neck right up to the wire and it meant a lot to me that I kept my game together to the very end.

On the way to victory in the World Match Play final – one of the high spots in the golden autumn of '87

15

What the Ryder Cup means to me

I have purposely not said anything about the Ryder Cup so far, as that has been an extraordinary experience and in some ways totally divorced from all the other golf I have played. Normal tournament play builds up to a climax during the last round and over the closing holes. The Ryder Cup, especially now that we are playing the Americans on even terms, is almost the reverse – the greatest pressure is on the 1st tee, though of course, it never lets up.

I first played in 1983, which was also Tony Jacklin's first year as Captain. Never have I been so nervous on the 1st tee – I felt physically sick. My first

With Sam Torrance in my first Ryder Cup – on the first hole, Sam could only advise!

Four years later with Nick Faldo at Muirfield Village

game was in a four-ball on the afternoon of the first day and Sam Torrance was my partner. He saw how nervous I was and casually said he'd look after things till I got into the match. Naturally he drove first for us – and hit it out of bounds! It was three or four holes before HE got into the match, but we managed to halve the game. Apart from that, I didn't play all that well, but the experience stood me in good stead for the next two contests.

To have been part of that great winning sequence, and particularly the first away win at Muirfield Village, is something that I expect will only be surpassed by my first victory in a major championship.

In all other golf, some of the pleasure and satisfaction can be measured in pounds, shillings and pence. But to be a member of a winning Ryder Cup team is something any golfer should be prepared to walk across broken glass for.

17

2 The Power Game

I have never been much of a reader of instructional books on golf or follower of articles on how to play the game. If I had been, I doubt I would have achieved what I have done. This is because, while I was growing up in golf, it seemed that unless you were six foot tall and swung the club up over your head, you had no chance to compete with the best. Ideas have changed now.

This upright swing was made possible by a dramatic increase in the fitness and strength of the top golfers. It enabled them to develop swings which kept the club face square to the ball throughout the swing and still hit it far enough to cope with the longest golf courses. The theory behind this was to eliminate the rolling clubface as it came into the ball and thereby cut out one of the variables of the golf swing. It was achieved not only by a much steeper swing, but also by almost entirely cutting out wrist action.

This was initially called the square-to-square method and its most notable exponent was Jack Nicklaus. Today, the golfer who comes nearest to playing this way is Greg Norman, though his position at the top of his backswing is considerably flatter than that of the young Nicklaus.

This was fine if you were young, tall and strong, and it significantly increased the gap between the top professionals and the rest of the golf playing world – though that didn't stop many people trying to emulate the pros and probably caused a few back problems into the bargain.

There were exceptions and the most obvious would have to be Gary Player, who by the standards of those days swung pretty flat. Not even his best friend would say he had a great swing, but he got there by an almost manic determination and a magical short game.

It was a time when golfers were seeking to find and perfect a repeating golf swing, to carry them through even the most nerve-racking moments. They sought to achieve this by building factors into their swings to cut out error. The result of this was a reduction of moving parts throughout the swing.

The upright swing they all used in the '60s and '70s: Jack Nicklaus (left) *and Greg Norman* (right)

All this built tension and rigidity into a lot of swings. This may reduce the worst results of bad shots, but at the expense of distance. This didn't matter to the big boys as their increased athleticism, allied to the improvements in golfing equipment, meant that they could hit the ball far enough most of the time.

You may wonder where all this is leading. Well, if I had to come up with one factor that enables me to hit the ball so far, it is the *lack* of tension and rigidity in my swing. It is what I don't do, rather than what I do do, that is the secret. The result is a balance and rhythm that has been allowed to develop naturally.

Getting set up

Like many things in life, if you don't start correctly, you have little chance of doing a good job. Always remember, though, that taking up your position to hit the ball – the address – is not a static thing. The moment you stand completely still, you will have created tension. The more tension there is, the more likely you are to hit a bad shot, as well as lose distance. Let's look at the elements of the set-up.

The Grip

Everyone's instinct is to grip the club in such a way that they feel will enable them to hit the ball as far as possible. The result of this is usually too 'strong' a grip – the left hand too far over the top and the right one too far under. The perfect combination for a searing hook!

With my grip, I try to place the hands on the shaft of the club in such a way as to bring the club face back to the ball square every time. Distance, as we shall see, comes from getting other things right.

There is no such thing as the perfect grip because the size and shape of everyone's hands are different and above all the grip must be comfortable. There are, however, a few principles that must be adhered to.

The left hand

In placing the club in the left hand, the shaft should run from the middle joint of the forefinger to the 'heel' of the hand. Provided the thickness of the grip is right for you, a matter I shall touch on when discussing equipment,

The Woosnam grip – the back of the left hand and the palm of the right towards the hole

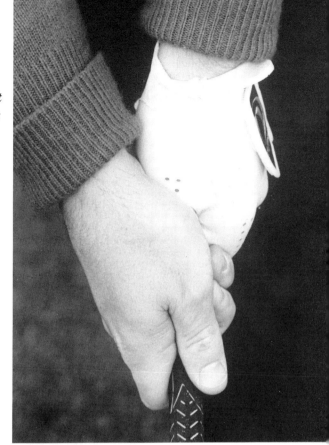

Below left: *The clubshaft should be across the palm of the left hand but in the fingers of the right. Note the Gripright grip to check hand position*

Below right: *No more than one and a half knuckles showing, and the thumb on the top of the shaft*

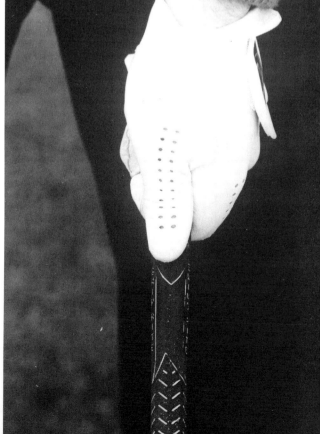

this will place the thumb just over the top of the shaft, when the hand is closed.

If you haven't been doing this, it will probably feel very weak to start with, but it is essential to persevere and the reward will be greater consistency.

The right hand

Much has been written about the options available, what with the overlapping, the interlocking and the two-handed grips. Which of these is right for you depends mainly on the size of your hands and, in the end, what is most comfortable. The reason for doing something *other* than grip the club with all the fingers of both hands on the shaft is to make the hands work together as one and, at the same time, reduce the imbalance of strength between right and left.

In simple terms, if you have very small hands, then a two-fisted grip is acceptable, as anything else will make it difficult to hang on to the club. My fellow-countryman, Dai Rees, played throughout his career this way and he didn't do too badly. He even allowed the club to move in his right hand as well!

Of the other grips, overlapping – the Vardon – is far and away the most popular, though the interlocking has its fans, particularly amongst those with hands on the smallish side. For the first half of his career, Nicklaus gripped this way.

Left: *Pretty orthodox – the Vardon (or Taylor, depending on whom you read) grip*. Right: *The interlocking grip, as favoured by Nicklaus for many years*

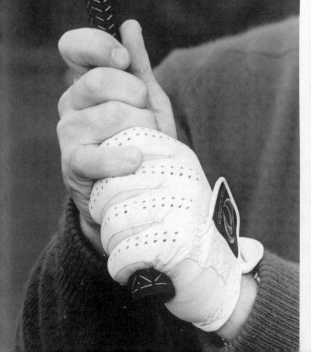 

The best known exponent of the two-fisted grip – the late Dai Rees

For myself, with an overlapping grip, the palm of the right hand fits neatly over the left-hand thumb, with the groove formed between the thumb and the forefinger pointing at the right shoulder. The right hand grips the club more in the fingers than does the left and this is where the feel and control come from. It is important to keep a regular check on the grip, as it can easily slip out of line. Whilst it might seem elementary for a top pro, I prefer to use a 'griprite' grip, which has the positions for the thumbs marked on it in just the right place. You would be surprised how many of us use this grip.

Not only can the grip change with the passage of time, it can also shift during a round. In great heat, or under a lot of pressure, the palms become slippery with perspiration and there is a tendency to grip tighter, causing the left hand to creep over to the right, into the 'strong' position. Suddenly you could be hooking the ball or even blocking it out to the right.

The Stance

For all full shots, my stance is the same width as my shoulders, and whether you are tall and slim, short and wide, or any other combination, this is a good principle. Too narrow and you will have trouble balancing; too wide and you won't be able to use your legs properly.

The knees should be lightly flexed – not bent as this again implies being fixed in one position and therefore rigidity. The back should be straight, keeping the head up and as far away from the ball as possible. This will ensure the shoulders are free to turn fully and not hunched up into the neck, as can often happen under pressure.

I keep my weight perhaps 60 per cent on my heels, thus providing a solid base and enabling me to keep the club on the inside until after I have hit the ball. If I have my weight too far forward – on my toes – this causes me to swing too steeply, with a resultant loss of power.

For every shot, long or short, I address the ball from the same spot, just back of the left heel. With the shorter shots, the stance narrows, but the ball stays in the same place.

In deciding how far to stand from the ball, here more than anywhere it is comfort that dictates. You should not be reaching for the ball, nor should you be tucked up in yourself. The arms should hang a little forward of vertically down from the shoulders and this again will give you room to stay on the inside of the ball, on both backswing and downswing. Obviously, the shorter the club, the nearer the ball you will stand.

The feet (well at least the heels!) the same width as the shoulders

Comfortable at the address, knees flexed and back straight – neither reaching for the ball, nor too close

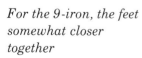

For the 9-iron, the feet somewhat closer together

My address routine

Every golfer should have a routine he goes through just prior to hitting the ball. This will be rehearsed on the practice ground and in friendly rounds, in fact, whenever he's hitting a golf shot, and will thus become totally automatic. When the crunch comes and you are faced with a critical shot and the brain becomes numb, auto pilot will take over, the routine will be the same and so will the swing.

I start with the club in my right hand and place it so that the face is pointing directly at the target. Using the right hand for this keeps me slightly 'open' and looking down the line of the shot. It also helps put my body in the right position, with the right shoulder lower than the left.

I like to feel that I am slightly open at the address, that is with the shoulders and hips facing just left of the target. The way I hit the ball, this puts me in position to have the left side of the body moving out of the way by the time the clubhead gets back to the ball.

The mind is a powerful force and it determines our physical actions. It is therefore very important to have a clear, mental picture of the shot you are going to play. If you really can 'see' a shot, it's amazing how often you bring it off.

Before taking the club away, I pick a spot on the back of the ball, the number perhaps, and look at that. That makes sure that my head stays behind the ball, throughout the swing.

How I hit the ball

As I said at the beginning, one of the secrets of whatever success I have had is that I have never tried to analyse deeply all the separate elements that go to make up the golf swing. To me, a golf swing is a flowing whole and the moment you start thinking of it in fragments, that's when rhythm and timing go out the window.

In telling you how I hit the ball, I will be concentrating on those relatively few things that I think are important when making a golf swing and which for me are the fundamentals that make the whole thing work.

Opposite above: *Choose a set-up routine and stick with it. For me, position the clubhead with the right hand, apply the left and then take up the stance.*
Below: *This leaves me slightly open at the address*

Somewhat different in height! – but arms about the same length

Although I'm not much over 5 feet 4 inches, my arms are about the same length as those of say, Nick Faldo or Sandy Lyle. I would also use clubs of approximately the same length and therefore have all the ingredients for just as wide an arc as those taller fellows.

Width of arc is certainly one of the important ingredients of long hitting. Also, being shorter and consequently standing more upright than they, my shoulders and hips move in an almost identical plane, therefore working much more together than in a taller man. They, on the other hand, find their shoulders moving more up and down, while their hips spin on a lateral plane.

This, together with good rhythm and timing, is perhaps the single ingredient that enables me to keep up with and often pass much taller players.

My backswing

The foundation of a wide arc and good rhythm is a low, slow takeaway. The lower the club stays to the ground over the first 3 or 4 feet, the wider will be the arc. In stretching to keep the club low, this automatically begins the vital transfer of weight over to the right side and this in itself increases the width.

Keep the clubhead low to the ground for as long as possible and start to transfer the weight to the right side

*See how the
head stays
still
throughout,
no bobbing up
and down*

With all these factors pulling the body to the right, it is critical that the one thing to stay in place is the head. That said, a tiny movement right is no disaster – it is at least keeping the head behind the ball throughout and that's critical.

What *is* vital is that the head doesn't bob up and down. It is very easy when going for a low wide arc, to allow the head to drop on the backswing.

A good check on head movement during the swing is, when practising, to place one of those tilting shaving mirrors on the ground beyond the ball. Then watch yourself, while swinging. It's quite easy to look in the mirror and hit the ball at the same time and you will see if your head is moving and in what direction.

The start of the backswing cannot be too slow. The backswing is after all just a matter of putting the club and body in the right position to knock the ball in the direction you want it to go. Rush this part, as many people do either all the time, or under the stress of competition, and all the energy necessary to propel the ball as far as possible is wasted in the wrong part of the swing.

By stating this, I do not mean to imply that the backswing is a self-contained thing on its own, and everything comes to a halt when it is complete. As you know when watching slow motion replays on the television, parts of the body – legs and hips for example – are already starting the forward part of the swing, while the club and hands are still getting to the top of the backswing. No. All I am trying to point out is that a lot of energy spent getting the club back requires energy to stop it when it gets there. So this braking energy cannot then be used for its proper purpose of creating the maximum amount of clubhead speed where it's most needed – at the moment of impact.

So, having started the swing slowly to achieve a gradual build-up to full speed when back at the ball, and low to get the maximum width, I then concentrate on turning my back to the target. I do not think of anything else. To have good rhythm and a flowing swing the club and hands must go naturally to the top of the backswing. I don't think this is necessarily as difficult as many people make out.

Think for a moment that golf was just a one-handed, right-handed game (left, if left-handed). Imagine that you are walking through a field of barley, just about the time of the harvest, and have in your hands a light stick. You would see nothing difficult in flicking off an ear of barley here and there as you walked by. Stand still for a moment and take a full swing, to try and knock off as many as possible. That wouldn't be too difficult? Well, that is exactly what the right-hand side of the body does, when hitting a golf ball. In a sporting context, it is also very similar to hitting a squash ball, which has bounced approximately knee high.

The reason I say it is natural for the hands and club to go to the right position, is because when you carry out the actions described above, you don't swing the racket or stick around your bum or up over your head. It goes somewhere in between. That somewhere is pretty well where the top of the backswing should be. Depending on your height, it will naturally be much higher and above the shoulders, if you are tall. If, like me you are a bit shorter, then the arc will be much lower, and round the shoulders. Try it.

Ah, I hear you say, but the golf ball isn't sitting where the ear of barley or the bouncing squash ball are. No, but you have a longer stick to hit it with and you are after all bending over a bit to compensate for the object being on the ground. All I am trying to do is to give you, through another, more easily visualized, physical action, an appreciation of what a good golf swing should feel like, at least with the right side of the body.

I also agree that to do it with two hands on the club or racket is much more difficult. But if you put the left hand on the club as described when gripping it, and keep it in a passive role, allowing the right hand to dictate, then you could start to get the semblance of a good natural swing.

Another important lesson to be learnt, from the examples described above, is that the very action of knocking off an ear of barley or hitting a squash ball, is exactly how you should hit a golf ball. When performing these actions, the stick or racket is left behind as you come into the hitting area and whipped through at the last moment. That's what you do with a golf shot.

So far, when talking about the backswing, I have only mentioned the upper part of the body. So let's go back to the address position and deal with the lower part.

There you were standing at the ball with the knees lightly flexed. With the wide arc, the weight was being transferred over to the right side. At the top of the backswing, perhaps 80 per cent of the weight will be on the right leg.

The one thing I concentrate on as regards the legs during the backswing is that the knees stay flexed throughout, particularly the right one. This will go a long way to ensuring that you do not overswing. If you keep the right knee always slightly bent, this limits the amount that the hips can turn, which then dictates how far round the shoulders go. To accommodate this, you will find that the left knee will bend more and move inwards towards the right knee, bringing the left heel off the ground. That's fine. It keeps it loose and not inhibiting any of the other moving parts of the body.

Get all these things right, plus make certain that you continue to hang on to the club throughout – no flute playing – and keep an almost straight left arm and the club of its own accord will be just about in the right position. You will notice that I do not talk about a TOTALLY straight left arm. This is deliberate, as once again, anything as strict as that will introduce rigidity into the swing. Above all, that is what I want to avoid. Also if you have concentrated on the maximum width of swing, you will automatically have a pretty straight left arm.

Left: *Note the difference stature makes. I'm fairly upright, with the weight more on the heels*

Right: *Nick Faldo, knees more bent, the top half of the body over the ball and weight more on the toes*

Above: *Watch that you don't let go with the left hand at the top of the backswing. . .*

. . . as a great golfer from another era used to, Harold Hilton

The clubface in the 'neutral' position and the arms forming two sides of a triangle, with the club at the apex – might have given myself a better lie though!

I have also not mentioned anything about the angle of the clubface. This again is deliberate. You will see from the pictures that having got all the other elements right, the clubface is naturally in the neutral position, half-way between open and shut. You will also see that the back of the left hand and the clubface are in alignment. That is as they were at the start of the swing, so again that is the result of allowing the body to do what comes naturally.

Finally, notice how the hands are at the apex of what appears to be a perfect triangle, made by the two forearms. Once more it is the natural and most comfortable position, having got the basics right. Note too, that the club is pointing just to the left of the target, but on a parallel line to that between the ball and the flag.

What you see is just about the ideal position for the top of the backswing. Obviously things do go wrong and it takes years of practice and many thousands of golf shots to do this every time. There are, however, a couple of fundamental things to watch out for, when using a full shoulder turn and a rounded swing.

It is very easy, when concentrating on making a full shoulder turn, to overswing with the club shaft going beyond the horizontal. Provided you are hanging on to the club properly, this can only be caused by a straightening of the right leg, which starts to push the weight back towards the left, before you are ready for it.

Left: *A young Ben Crenshaw swinging way past the horizontal; greater consistency has come from a more curtailed backswing in recent years*

Right: *Of similar build to myself, Gary Player had a flatter swing than most*

It is also easy to swing flat. By 'flat' I mean that the hands and club are too low round the back as opposed to being up above the shoulders. This will be caused by turning the clubhead away from the ball too quickly at the start of the swing and the effect will be for the club to be pointing to the RIGHT of the target at the top of the backswing.

37

The downswing

The first movement you make from the top of the backswing determines the type of shot you are going to hit. I concentrate on pulling down as hard as I can with my left hand. This does two things. It starts the weight shifting back towards the left side of the body and ensures that the club stays inside the line of the shot to the target.

As with so many parts of the golf swing, the weight shift has to be an almost instinctive and natural part of the whole. By pulling down with the left hand, the left shoulder starts to come up and turn away and that effect in itself starts the reverse weight transfer.

In an ideal world, the downswing will mirror the path of the backswing. It will be somewhat inside the wide arc going back, caused by the angle of the shaft to the arms being much more acute. In effect the angle between shaft and forearms will be the same as it was at the top of the backswing, until the hands release the clubhead at the ball in the hitting area.

The start of the downswing, and the weight starts to shift to the left

Note how much narrower the arc of the downswing (below) *is compared with the backswing* (above)

The hands lead all the way back to the ball

Here again is a crucial element in hitting the ball a long way. This late release of the clubhead causes a flail or whiplash effect that dramatically increases the clubhead speed at the moment of impact. Remember the one-handed swing at the barley or squash ball? Try doing that with a firm wrist, as in a forehand at tennis and you will notice how much harder it is to achieve the same speed – even if you can.

From the days of the early Jack Nicklaus and the big strong golfers, it was believed if you could cut out this flail action, you would eliminate one of the variables that produces crooked shots. Much of the teaching over the past twenty years has been aimed at that, particularly among the top professionals and it is only recently that most are now reverting to the flatter swing and the late hit, which is how the game always used to be played. The classic example of this change has been the highly visible endeavour of Nick Faldo to remodel his swing – but that is the subject of another, and probably longer, book than this.

The downswing, the hitting of the golf ball and the follow-through all have to be one continuous flowing movement. The process is started by pulling down with the left hand, but once the weight transfer from right to left has begun, and the club is travelling inside the line of the shot, then the right hand and side take over. It is now impossible to go 'over the top', ie. throw the club outside the line, with all the many horrors that that can produce – slice, smothered hook and, worst of all, the dreaded shank.

In the impact zone

Whilst taking you through the various stages of the golf swing, I must emphasize that it is vital not to think of it as a collection of bits and pieces. With the skill of the photographer to stop the swing at every point, it is tempting to select positions you would like to be in at certain points. This is fatal, since it will make your swing stiff and stilted, the very factors that will inhibit your ability to hit the ball a long way – or straight. These good positions are a result of doing things correctly earlier in the swing cycle.

In hitting the ball, I am conscious of keeping my head behind the ball until it's on its way, of hitting hard with the right hand and keeping the club low to the ground for as long as possible after the strike. Until the ball has been hit, the right elbow stays close in to the body.

Head down and behind the ball till well after impact

My natural line of swing is from inside to out, till well after the ball has been dispatched. . . .

Having started the downswing on the inside, this will be continued through to the ball, the natural line of the swing moving outside the line of flight only after the ball has been struck. This, combined with natural closing of the clubface to the moment of impact, is what imparts the right-to-left spin and causes the draw, which is the ideal shape for greater distance.

Whilst this is going on, the body is in the midst of a full 180-degree turn, around the imaginary stake stuck through the top of the head and coming out at the base of the spine. As the arms, hands and club come into the ball, the left side is busy getting out of the way to allow the right side to come through after impact.

42

The follow-through

It has often been difficult for the handicap golfer to grasp the importance of the follow-through. Logic says that once the ball has gone, what you then do can have no effect on it. That of course is true, but, as we have seen, everything we do in our golf swing is the result of what has happened earlier. If we were to stop everything immediately after the ball has been hit – and I've seen quite a few who do just that – that stopping process will have started long before the club gets to the ball with all the detrimental effects that this involves. Therefore, a full follow-through is only the natural result of doing everything else right beforehand.

In talking about hitting the ball, I mentioned how I think of keeping the club low to the ground for as long as possible after the strike. The way I swing the club, the bottom, the low point of the swing, is a few inches beyond the ball. This is not so obvious with a driver or even the other wooden clubs, but with the irons, the ball is always struck first and the divot comes out of the ground just beyond where the ball lay. Bearing in mind that the ball sits opposite the left foot at the address, you can see how instinct could start you coming up from the shot too soon.

. . . . and the clubhead stays low to the ground, for as long as possible after the hit

No one keeps their head down longer, or the club lower to the ground after impact, than Lee Trevino

The greatest exponent of staying low through and beyond the ball is Lee Trevino. I would not recommend you try and copy what he does, but one of the results of his looped, swaying swing is that he keeps the clubface square to the line of flight of the ball longer than any other top golfer today. Watch him at the Open Championship and you will see what I mean.

Remember that I regard the hitting of a golf ball as very much a right hand and side exercise. For me, the way to achieve this extension through the ball is to imagine the follow-through to be like the finish of throwing a discus. In that sport, your right arm is always fully extended until right at the top of the follow-through.

From all that has gone before, you might think that I totally disregard the left side of the body. This is not true. As the right side carried all the weight at the top of the backswing, so throughout the downswing and follow-through, that weight transfers to the left side, until more than 90 per cent

44

The finish of the swing, with the weight now almost totally on the left side

will be on the left side at the finish. That transfer is perhaps the most important factor in enabling me to keep the clubhead low after hitting the ball.

Also, the left arm and side are the stanchion, the pillar that enables me to hit the ball as hard as I can without fear of hooking. Were the left arm to bend at, or immediately after, the moment of impact and the left side collapse, then the right hand would whip the club through too quickly. The in-to-out line of the swing would become in-to-in and the low, wide follow-through would never happen.

The correct position at the completion of the swing features the hands high, the chest pointing at the target and the weight almost totally on the left foot. Above all, balance must be maintained – no sense of topple or walking after the ball. Even this will be a sign that all was not perfect during the swing.

Summary

So to summarize; if I had to pick out what I believe to be the factors that contribute to hitting the ball a long way, certainly for me, they would be as follows:

Eliminate tension from the swing at all times

So many, when trying for the big one, tense up. They seem to believe by gripping the club tighter, hunching the shoulders and lashing the ball for all its worth, they will hit the really big one. All this does is make the swing rigid and removes the elasticity so essential in good rhythm and timing. The upper half of the body becomes glued together, with the various parts unable to do their individual jobs.

Just remember how often you have swung easily at the ball, perhaps believing you have too much club, and hit the best shot of the day – miles over the target. So relax, be loose and concentrate on tempo to achieve a better quality of strike. Extra distance will be just one of the benefits that will accrue.

Width of arc

Provided the rhythm and timing are correct, the further the clubhead travels, the more speed it will pick up. And the wider the arc, the further the clubhead goes. To achieve this, keep the clubhead low to the ground for as long as possible – almost feeling to stretch the club away from you. Take care though not to overdo this and allow the head to duck down.

Done correctly this will lead to:

Transfer of weight (mark 1)

Used correctly, the body weight can be added to the impetus of the shot at the moment of impact, by travelling in the direction of the shot. To make this happen, the weight must first be taken away from the target, by shifting it onto the right side during the backswing. At the top of the backswing, some 80 per cent of your weight should be on the right foot.

Watch out though. The dividing line between transferring the weight correctly and swaying away is very fine. Control this by making sure that the head stays virtually static, hardly moving away from where it was at the address position.

Hips and shoulders move in the same plane

To hit the ball a long way, everything must be working together. With my swing, the hips and shoulders move very much in the same plane and this enables the big back muscles to be devoted fully to the production of the shot. Where, particularly on taller people, the shoulders tilt more in the vertical, while the hips revolve horizontally, those same muscles are being pulled this way and that by the various parts of the body moving in different directions.

Squash shot action of the right hand and wrist

I developed this type of action when trying to keep up with my elders as a young lad. It is really a rolling of the hands into the ball, so that the clubface moves from open to shut during the process of hitting the ball. The danger of this is that the tiniest loss of precision can mean a sharp hook or slice. Thousands of hours of practice have reduced the errors to a minimum and I now have tremendous confidence that it will work, even under the direst pressure.

In effect, it makes the striking of the ball a right-hand dominated shot. The left acts as control, ensuring that the right doesn't overtake the left until after the ball is on its way.

Transfer of weight (mark 2)

We left the weight 80 per cent on the right side at the top of the backswing. Through the downswing, the striking of the ball and on to the completion of the follow-through, the weight moves across to the other – the left – side. Get this right, and it almost has to be instinctive, and all your weight will be added to the power of the shot, giving those exciting extra yards. At the completion of the swing, 80 per cent of your weight should be on the left foot.

This can only be got right by:

The Woosnam swing

The correct use of the legs

I see the swing as being rather like the winding and unwinding of a watch spring. At the top of the backswing, you are fully wound. From there, the legs are the leading element of the unravelling process. They are the first part of the body that starts the move back towards the target, and perhaps even begin to while the hands and the club are still completing the backswing. A good leg action, pulling the rest of the swing after it, is vital to long hitting and no one ever hit the ball a long way without a strong pair of legs.

If you can maximize these elements of your golf swing then extra distance will follow. Above all though it is the timing and the rhythm that are so important – strike the ball better and you will hit it further. When you see the best in the world in action on the television, try and capture the pace of some of the classic swingers – Seve or Curtis Strange – and take it with you to the practice ground. It will help you find that elusive thing – the perfect strike.

3 The Commercial Game

Hitting the ball a long way off the tee or smashing a fairway wood 260 yards to the heart of a par 5 is great fun, but it is still only a small part of the game of golf. Golf has many faces, psychological as well as physical, and all these have to be understood if you are to become a competent golfer or, as in my case, make a living at the game. Let's start by looking at all the other ingredients of the long game – everything concerned in getting the ball onto or near the putting surface.

Through the bag

It is important to understand how the swing changes depending on which club you have in your hand. In the search for consistency, it is vital to change as few things as possible, when making a full swing at the ball.

Whatever the club, always be comfortable at the address. As the shaft gets shorter, so I stand nearer the ball

In simple terms, the shorter the club, the nearer to the ball I stand and the narrower the stance becomes. The routine, the grip and above all the tempo of the swing are all the same. The swing naturally becomes more upright and the arc narrower, the nearer the ball I stand. The angle of attack into the ball becomes steeper and that is the prime reason for the deeper-faced clubs putting so much more backspin on the ball than the longer irons.

There is one other fundamental change. The shorter the club, the shorter the swing. At the top of the backswing with a 9-iron or wedge, the club is not all that much past the vertical and nowhere near the horizontal, as with the driver.

So, the shorter the club, the smaller everything becomes.

The shorter the shaft, the shorter the backswing

Safety from the tee

There are many occasions, whether you be professional or amateur, when the dangers off the tee outweigh the need to hit the ball a long way. Amongst the televised golf holes in Great Britain, the 17th on the West course at Wentworth springs to mind with its bulging out of bounds up the left-hand side. All tournament players have a plan when it comes to safety first and you should too.

In professional golf, the 1-iron has become the instrument of safety, allied to a slight and acceptable loss of distance. For Mr Average Golfer, this would be like changing one nightmare for another, the long iron being perhaps the most difficult instrument in the bag to use. However, the principle ought to be adopted and you should become familiar with hitting a 3- or 4-wood from the tee for just these occasions. Not only are these clubs much easier to use than the driver, particularly off a low tee, but their higher trajectory means less run on the ball and the crooked shot gets into less trouble.

This last fact, by itself, will breed more confidence over a period of time and you will be surprised how accurate you can become with these more friendly clubs from the tee. It is also a good alternative to have up your sleeve, should your driving desert you at any time.

Some people's swings are, however, more suited to the steeper angle of attack of the long iron, than the shallow sweep with a 3- or 4-wood. Often, perhaps purely psychologically, they feel more in control with an iron than a wood, and even though the 1-iron would be beyond them, a 2, 3 or 4 would do just as well. Shorter par 4s often offer opportunities for sensible safety play, without putting too great a stress on the second shot and a club or two extra is a small price to pay for the bonus of being certain of playing the second shot from the fairway.

One word of warning. In taking a longish iron from the tee, be sure to pick a spot to aim at on the fairway within the range of the club selected. It is a natural reaction to take an iron for safety and then undo all the good work by lashing at the ball to make up the distance sacrificed. The subconscious sometimes sees the fairway as a much larger target than the green and that any old shot will do. Picture the shot as being to a flag on a short hole green and play accordingly.

While on the subject of long irons and the difficulty many people find in playing them, it is true that there is less margin for error than with a 3- or 4-wood or a medium iron. This knowledge, in itself, causes a lot of golfers to tense up with a long iron in their hand and often the result of that tension is to try and hit too hard and swing too quickly. To get more comfortable with those clubs in the bag, which if you really connect can give more pleasure than almost any other, try playing them as though you were attempting a long pitch – an easy half to three-quarter swing – taking perhaps a club or two more than you normally would for a given distance. Concentrate on a precise, clean strike and let the distance take care of itself.

Judging distance

In the last chapter, we saw the need for a repeating swing if the ball was to be sent in the right direction every time. With shots to the green there is an added dimension. I need to know exactly how far I hit the ball with each club in the bag and I need to hit it that distance every time. What is more important, is that I must *believe* I will hit it that distance, if I am to have total confidence every time I step up to hit a shot to the green.

In the old days, even the very best golfers used to use judgment of eye and feel when selecting a club and then deciding how hard to hit it. Nowadays, with the enormous competition in professional golf, nothing must be left to chance, which is why we pace out every hole we ever play. This way, we can come to a new course every week and play it confidently after only one or two practice rounds. Even then, we still have to go back to the old skills from time to time. Yardage charts go out the window when the wind blows at the seaside, as in recent Open Championships! That said, knowing the distance left still underpins the confidence, even though we might be having to play a 1-iron where we might normally hit a 7 downwind.

Now I am not suggesting that you need to acquire this degree of precision or that you will ever have the time or inclination to do so. But there is something for you to learn from it, which could benefit your game. Next time you play a round of golf, look back to your dropped shots and see how many of them were the result of misjudgment of distance. You will be surprised at the answer.

A little attention to this area of the game could well cut a few shots off your handicap. Go onto the practice ground and hit a number of shots – say 15 or 20 with one club. The good ones should all be within 10 or 12 yards of one another. Pace off the distance to the centre of the bunch and that will give you a pretty good idea of how far you hit the ball with that club. Repeat the exercise with each club and then you have a distance dossier on your golf game. Next, do what we do and pace out your course.

You will still make mistakes, as you won't hit the ball with the consistency that we do. However, you might be surprised how much more confident you feel, knowing that you've got the right club in your hand.

Backspin

So much of golf is about confidence and confidence comes from knowing, or at least strongly believing, what is going to happen when you hit the ball. Doubt is the great destroyer of the game. As we have seen, judgment of distance is about knowing how far you hit the ball with each club and also knowing how far you have got to go with the next shot. It is also important to know what is going to happen when the ball gets to where you hit it.

It is fair to say that if you make good contact with the ball with any iron club, you will get a degree of backspin. The straighter the clubface – ie. the 2- or 3-iron – the less that backspin will be. If there is such a person as the average golfer, then he will make good contact with the longer irons so rarely, that it is better to assume he will impart no backspin. In which case he should not go for the green with such a club, unless he can pitch some 20 to 30 yards before it and let the ball run on. Much better to use the 4- or 5-wood, where the angle of descent is much greater and so there is less forward momentum when the ball lands.

One problem with backspin comes at the other end of the club range. With the 9-irons, and wedges too, it screws back 15 or 20 yards, having pitched by the pin. In other words, too much backspin. With the shorter clubs and the steeper angle of attack, the harder you hit the ball, the faster the ball runs back up the face of the club and the more spin is imparted. Where this is a real problem, say with a shot to a green sloping sharply towards you, the solution is to take a bigger club and hit it more softly.

With every course we play, as well as pacing it out for distance, we look carefully at the greens and the surrounding areas to see how they will respond to shots hit to them. This again will dictate how we plan our way round a course – where to attack and where to be cautious.

Designer shots

One of the fascinating things about golf is that it is not perfectable. Think how dull it would be if players got so good that they never hit a loose or crooked shot. We all have a few rounds where nothing much goes wrong and they are a great pleasure, but, much more often, we will hit a number of

The set-up and swing for a fade. Everything the same, except body positioned left with the clubface open – facing the target. The swing, as for a normal shot, but hitting the ball a glancing blow with that open clubface

shots that land us in trouble. When we do, we've got to get out of it as best we can.

Crooked shots often land you behind things – trees or bushes – and you have to manufacture shots to get round, over or under them. One thing all good golfers learn, as they develop their skills, is how to 'shape' shots, to hit them high or low, fade or draw. Once again, the secret is to change as little as possible of the fundamental golf swing.

The fade (or intentional slice)

Place the clubhead behind the ball facing directly at the target, even though that may be straight into the offending tree or bush. Then take up your stance with the left foot 4 to 6 inches further back than the right one. At the same time make sure that your shoulders are in alignment with your feet and the whole of your body will be pointing some 15 to 20 degrees to the left of the target. The ball will still be opposite the same point of the left foot as in the normal address position.

You now make a normal swing, though the plane will be from outside the line to the target on the backswing, to inside it on the follow-through. The ball will start off to the left and move back to the right as it approaches the target. As you are in effect addressing the ball with the clubface open, this will make you hit the ball higher than normal with that club and consequently not so far. You should therefore take one club more – say a 3-iron rather than a 4 – than you would normally take for a shot of that distance.

The draw (or intentional hook)

This is very much the reverse procedure to that for the fade. The clubface should be placed behind the ball, pointing directly at the target. This time the left foot should be 4 to 6 inches ahead of the right one, with the ball once again opposite the same part of the left foot. The shoulders are again aligned with the direction of the feet and the whole body pointing to the right of the target. Swing as normal, though the plane this time will be from inside to outside the line to the target.

The closed clubface position will this time have the effect of hitting the ball lower and therefore further, so one club less should be used to achieve the desired distance. Also, it is almost impossible to hit the ball from right to left and still achieve much backspin – Bobby Locke was the only man capable of doing that – so take that into your calculations when planning the shot.

For a draw, the reverse. The body set up to hit the ball to the right of target with the clubface closed

There is one other thing to remember when planning to shape a shot. The more loft the club has, the harder it is to impart side spin. So, if you have only a little over 100 yards to go, use a 6- or 7-iron and play your controlled hook or slice like a long pitch shot.

Hit it high

Occasionally, we want to hit the ball higher than the normal trajectory for a given club. It may be that we have something to go over or that we want the ball to land softly when it gets to the target. The easy solution might be to take a more lofted club, but that is going to mean a reduction in distance and that might be unacceptable.

*To hit the ball high,
move the ball forward
in the stance*

Still using the same fundamental swing, it is possible to hit the ball higher by moving the ball forward in the stance, to opposite the left toe, and by keeping the weight more on the right side throughout the swing. Keep the face of the club pointing at the target, even though this will make it appear slightly open. This will be compensated for by the strike being later in the swing and the club will be moving back inside the line of flight.

Remember that, with iron clubs in particular, the bottom of the swing is some 4 to 6 inches past where the club meets the ball. All we are doing here is to put that point of contact later in the swing cycle, in fact at the very bottom of the swing. This way we ensure that the full angle of the clubface is delivered to the ball, rather than the closed-over effect when a normal iron shot is hit. Note also, as we are now hitting the ball at the bottom of the swing and we want a clean contact with the ball, there will be little or no divot with this shot.

59

Hit it low

Not surprisingly, the change here is to move the ball further back in the stance, to somewhere nearer the mid point between the feet. Still keep the clubface aiming directly at the target, though this will give you the impression that it is more closed, hooded, than for a normal shot. The weight will, if anything, be more to the left side throughout the shot.

One of the factors that sends a golf ball up in the air is backspin. The harder you hit the ball, the more backspin is imparted. Therefore to keep the ball low, you want to hit it quite softly. The answer is to take a bigger club than you would normally need for the distance of shot, grip the club down the shaft and use a three-quarter swing. Again, more like a long pitch. This way the ball will stay low and you will have much more feeling of control.

Clubhead back in the stance to keep it low

Slopes

Very few golf courses are completely flat, one of the features that so often makes playing the game a joyous visual experience. However, it does from time to time complicate the act of striking a golf ball. Let's look at what we have to do when playing on the side of a hill.

Uphill
The natural instinct is to take a stance that will allow us to stand upright. In this case, it would mean standing with the left leg more bent than usual and the right one practically straight. If we then swing normally, all we will

With the ball on an up-slope, the angle of the shoulders and hips reflect that of the slope

do is drive the club into the side of the slope, with dire consequences for the shot, if not for the club and our hands!

The art is to get our body at the correct angle to the slope, though this of course instantly gives the feeling of falling back down the hill. To compensate for this, the hips should be moved forward at the address and allow the shoulders to reflect the uphill angle. Now make your normal swing, though the weight will stay further to the left, to keep you from toppling over.

This way the clubface will also reflect the slope and hit the ball higher and thus lose distance. The answer is to take a club or two more, grip down the shaft and play another of those three-quarter shots. This will again give a greater feeling of control at a time when balance is difficult.

Downhill

Again, the body should reflect the angle of the slope as far as possible and not fight it, although the weight should be balanced evenly, allowing the shoulders to be square to the slope.

On a down-slope, weight predominantly on the right side and clubface slightly open – and work really hard to keep the head behind the ball till after impact

One of the difficulties of this shot is to get the ball up in the air. So, open the face of the club slightly and aim left to accommodate the slice that this will produce. Once again, use your normal swing pattern. In the set up you've done all that is necessary to counteract the effects of the slope.

Standing below the ball
The natural contours will make you stand more erect at the address, as the ball will be level with some part of your shins. This is fine, but will result in your swing having a flatter plane than normal. The angle of the hill will make you feel like toppling backwards, and to compensate for this, your weight should be more forward, on your toes, than usual.

With the flatter swing, there is a tendency to draw the ball, so aim to the right to accommodate it. Balance is important, so keep the weight towards the toes throughout the shot, so as not to fall away from the shot.

Where the slope is pronounced, you will need to grip down the shaft, so as not to be pushed over backwards.

Standing below the ball, the stance will be more upright, the club can be gripped a little shorter and the swing will be a little flatter

With the ball below the feet, the weight must be more on the heels to compensate for the upper part of the body being more bent over. Allow for a fade as the swing will inevitably be out-to-in

Standing above the ball

The reverse of being below the ball, this will mean that your weight will be on your heels. To be able to put the club behind the ball, it is necessary to bend over the ball more than you normally would for a shot from flat ground. This will also mean that your feet will be nearer the ball for the length of club.

The weight will stay back on your heels throughout the shot and being close to the ball, you will tend to swing outside the line of flight, so aim left to allow for the resultant fade.

Getting out of trouble

The first law, as every young golfer is taught on his mother's knee, is to do whatever is necessary to get out of wherever you are, *first time*. The secret, and this only comes from experience, is to know what your capabilities are and play within them.

The rough

Time and again, I have seen golfers with no chance, or even intention of getting on the green, take a club which would require a miracle to move the ball from the spot it is in. It is natural to want to move the ball as near to the green as possible with every shot, but as it is going to take you two shots to get on the green anyway, use both of them wisely. The conservative stroke from a bad lie will only mean a club or two more for the next shot and a much better chance of not dropping further shots.

Always remember that from the rough, whether it be long grass or heather, you will have very little control over how the ball will fly. It may be that you can get a straight-faced club to the ball and still hit it quite well. The effect of the long grass or heather on the clubhead will often produce a sharp hook or slice, landing you in further trouble. So again, the shorter recovery shot may be best.

When playing from thick grass or heather, it is important to make as clean a contact with the ball as possible. A normal swing runs the risk of the clubhead getting caught up long before it gets to the ball, so a special type of shot is required.

When in deep trouble, open the clubface, as the rough will tend to close it for you

The short, sharp, crisp stroke needed to extricate a ball from deep rough

The ball should be addressed with the clubface slightly open to compensate for the inevitable shutting of the blade as the club enters the rough around the ball. The hands are distinctly in front of the clubhead at the address and stay that way throughout the swing. The club is picked up sharply on the backswing, thus creating a steep, narrow arc. This way, the angle of attack into the ball will be as acute as possible, with the clubhead coming into the ball nearer the vertical than for a normal golf shot. With the hands continuing to lead, the shot is a short, sharp blow, with a very restricted follow-through.

Finally, remember, you will get far less backspin out of rough, so the ball will run further on landing than if it is hit from the fairway. Occasionally, if the grass is damp and some strands get caught between the clubface and the ball at the moment of impact, a 'flyer' will result. This is a ball hit with virtually no backspin whatsoever and, as the word implies, the ball travels much further through the air than it would from the fairway. Trouble over and beyond the target can be just as bad, if not worse, than on either side or short.

Bunkers

I deal with greenside bunkers in the chapter on the short game, but there is a totally separate strategy for getting out of fairway bunkers where distance is just as important as escape. Naturally, as with rough, recovery is the first principle. The club chosen must have sufficient loft to do the job.

When there is any object, such as the face of a bunker, to get over, the temptation is to scoop at the ball to get it up quickly. For a successful, long-distance bunker shot, this must be resisted. Earlier, we have seen how the steeper the angle of descent into the ball, the more sharply it will rise. The same is true out of bunkers.

Place the ball further back in the stance than normal, in much the same way as for the shot into the wind. This will give you the feeling of driving the ball into the face of the bunker in front of you. You won't. The clubface should be square to the target and the ball hit with a three-quarter swing. Of prime importance is to hit the ball BEFORE the sand and in this you will be helped by the ball being set back in the stance. Provided you have taken a club with sufficient loft, the steeper than normal angle of attack will do the rest.

One final point. You have studs in your shoes to stop you sliding around when on grass, but these will not be much help in sand. Having taken your stance, wriggle your feet around to dig a couple of little pits to give yourself a firm base. This will make you feel more secure and give you more confidence to hit the shot.

All the above applies if you have a decent lie in the bunker. If you are plugged or in a poached egg, back to rule 1. Just get it out.

Restricted backswing

After a bad shot or an unkind bounce, I sometimes find myself in a position where I cannot make a full swing at the ball. There is an obstacle impeding the backswing. Usually it will be a bush, trunk of a tree or a branch. Sometimes, when you are near the limits of the course, it will be a fence or stone wall – like the wall behind the green at the Road Hole on the Old Course at St Andrews.

In these situations, it is easy to get flustered and angry – especially if bad luck played a part in getting you there in the first place. It is also tempting to blame fate for not putting you perhaps as little as a yard away, where you would have had a perfectly clear swing at the ball. All too often these shots are tackled with the golfer full of negative thoughts, just at a time when he needs all his wits about him to cope with a very difficult situation.

What you must do first is THINK. Decide carefully what you can achieve from the spot the ball is in. If your best endeavour will only move the ball a few yards, probably the best option is to take a penalty drop to a place where you can get a proper swing at the ball. At least the result will be guaranteed and you won't be that much worse off than if you achieve the best possible shot under the circumstances. Nothing is worse – or more encouraging for your opponent – than if you hack at the ball, and fail to move it, or hit it into worse trouble.

Having calmly assessed the percentages and decided that a shot is on, take as much time as is necessary to prepare for what is, after all, going to be an unnatural and awkward shot. Work out what is the maximum backswing you have and allow yourself several practice swings to get totally familiar with the feel of the much shorter movement. Most important of all, stay with the swing you've rehearsed when you play the shot in earnest. The almost irresistible temptation is to compensate for the reduction of backswing with a heave from the shoulders and so get the sort of distance with the club in your hand that you might expect with a full shot. Disaster. . . .

Remember, you cannot expect much in the way of distance from a shortened backswing. Resist the temptation, pick a target area which will give you the best position to play to the green and maybe even recover well enough to save the shot you looked like dropping.

4 The Short Game

It seems to me that ordinary club golfers are not really concerned with getting better at the game. Why else would they ignore the one area which offers so many opportunities for cutting shots off their score?

I'm sure that any survey of people who read instructional golf books will show that the vast majority, on getting a new book, turn to the chapters on how to hit the ball – the golf swing. The fascination of golf is hitting the ball further and straighter, finding the magic formula that will make you hit it, even for just a day, like Jack Nicklaus or whoever your hero is.

It is this knowledge that makes authors tuck those bits dealing with the short game towards the end of the book. It is also the reason that at most clubs vast acres are devoted to the practice ground, while very few have a practice green with bunkers around for the members to hone the short game. They know that the facility would hardly be used.

Even golfers who have got into single figures often seem to spend 90 per cent of the time they devote to practice, hitting long shots and virtually ignoring that part of the game which contributes nearly half the shots they hit in a round. The holy grail is the soaring drive or the low 1-iron, arrow straight into the wind. If the handicap comes down in the process, well, it is a pleasant bonus.

Always remember, the short game is the shock absorber of golf. It enables you to bounce back from mistakes made in the long game. An indifferent drive followed by a poor second shot can still become a par with a good chip and putt. It takes a lot of long, straight hitting through the green to make up for a sloppy pitch and three miserable putts!

If you want proof that it is the short game that really matters, think back over the championships of the world, the ones you've seen on television, and note those that have been won or lost on the outcome of a single short shot. Bob Tway and Larry Mize holing out from off the green in successive majors at the end of 1986 and the beginning of 1987 to defeat Greg Norman in the

US PGA and the Masters are recent examples. Seve's chip to the final green in the 1988 Open Championship to keep Nick Price at bay was scarcely less good. From history, Trevino comes to mind chipping in on the 71st hole at Muirfield in 1972 against Tony Jacklin. On the debit side, who can forget Doug Sanders' missed putt on the last green at St Andrews in 1970?

Obviously, when pitches, chips or even very long putts go in there is an element of luck, but those who regularly put the ball close to the flag hole out more often than those who don't. And remember, only hours of practice have enabled the Tways, Trevinos and Mizes of this world to play those delicate shots really well at critical points of their lives.

All this, I suspect, will only serve to confirm the feeling that the mysteries of the short game are only revealed to those who give their entire lives to

Bob Tway holing out at the 72nd hole to steal the USPGA from Greg Norman in 1986 and Larry Mize (opposite) *doing the same thing at Augusta the following spring*

golf; that lesser mortals should never really expect to take less than three to get down from off the putting surface. Most golfers regard the rolling of three shots into two, as one of the delightful uncertainties of this absorbing game – something that occasionally happens, but is really nothing to do with them. This of course is nonsense.

Part of the problem is that there is such a variety of shots and situations that go to make up the short game. What should you practise and why? The answer is much the same as with the long game. You are seeking to do something so often, it becomes second nature, but instead of grooving the swing, this time you are seeking to groove the feel. Just by hitting lots of pitch shots from different distances, you will begin to acquire a better judgment of distance – yardage charts are fine, but for the shorter shots, it is

the belief that you will instinctively get the distance right that matters. That will come if you spend time on it, and it will come quickly if, as I suspect, it is an area you've neglected.

There are fewer hard and fast rules than in the long game, as with most shots there is more than one way to play them and a choice of clubs with which to do so. I will give the basic structure and with a little work from you, your handicap should start to fall.

The short game consists of four types of shot. The pitch, the chip, the bunker shot and the putt. The last two are obvious enough. The basic difference between the others is that a pitch shot is played predominantly through the air, with as little roll as possible once it hits the green, whereas the chip is like an extended putt and is designed to run most of the way to the hole.

The common theme that runs throughout my golf game is as true around the green as it was for the long shots. Be relaxed and well balanced for every shot, and change as little as possible from one shot to another. The position of the ball in relation to the feet will generally stay the same and the stroke at the ball will be a miniaturised version of what I do on the long shots.

The pitch

I regard 'pitching' as any shot from less than the distance I would normally hit a full wedge – say 90 yards. Now before you all shout that you can hit a wedge further than that, let me say that 90 to 100 yards is about as far as you want to hit a wedge without thrashing at it. It is a precision club.

At the beginning of the last chapter, we saw how the swing becomes shorter and narrower with the shorter shafted clubs. What a lot of golfers fail to realize is that you do not try, either, to hit those clubs with the same clubhead speed as with a driver. Clubhead speed is built up gradually throughout the entire length of the golf swing, until the point of impact. With a shorter swing there is not the time or length to build up the same speed and you should not try to do so.

Many of you have watched limited over cricket through the years and in many instances fast bowlers are made to come in off a short run. You will have seen the inexperienced bowlers still trying to generate full pace off this short run. It almost always looks uncomfortable and forced – they're pressing. The old pros recognize this, cut down on the speed and concentrate on 'line and length'. So it should be with you. If you feel you have to thrash a wedge to get there, take a 9-iron instead and swing at the natural pace that the length of club dictates.

Seve's pitch to the last hole at Lytham. He made it look easy, but without doubt the shot of 1988

The pitch continues this process of reduction in the length and strength of the golf swing. In every way it is just a shorter version of the full thing. The ball is still placed opposite the left instep, the stance is still shoulder wide and the grip the same as for the long shots.

As mentioned before, the pitch is like a miniature golf shot, and like a full shot to a green it should sit down quickly on arrival. It must therefore have backspin and to achieve that, the ball must be firmly struck. But how is this to be achieved if you only have 40 or 50 yards to go? The answer is, the shorter the shot, the lower down the shaft you grip the club. Then you can still hit the ball nice and crisply, without it flying too far and still imparting a reasonable amount of backspin.

If handicap golfers have trouble with this shot, it is because they grip the club too near the top of the shaft and then waft the club at the ball, quitting at that vital moment of impact. Going down the shaft will give a marvellous feeling of clubhead control that does wonders for confidence with the shorter shots.

The top of the backswing for the pitch shot – never more than a three-quarter swing and grip down the shaft for greater control and authority

The main difference from the normal golf shot is that the club is picked up more quickly from the ball. This is a natural result of the hands being nearer the clubhead anyway, but it is exaggerated, with the hands being a much more dominant factor in the execution of the shot.

The nearer the green you are, the shorter the swing becomes and the less backspin is created. This is where knowledge of the putting surface – the speed of the greens, the firmness of the ground – is vital so as to know how the ball will react on landing. This knowledge is added to the good golfer's instinctive feel for distance, which in itself is not unlike the ability to judge how far to throw a ball a specific distance underarm. Certainly the way the right hand and wrist perform that task is not dissimilar to how they operate on a short golf shot.

All the foregoing relates to those situations when, as the saying goes, 'you

Position the ball forward to hit the high pitch (left) *and back to hit it in low*

have plenty of green to work with'. Many are the occasions though, when the pin is set close to one side of the green, there is a bunker to get over or the green slopes away from you. In these instances you need to cut back on the normal run of the ball, if you wish to get close to the pin. The only way to achieve this is to get the ball up quickly, so that it comes down straighter and with less forward momentum on it. For this a few things do have to be changed.

The ball should be a little further forward in the stance – just opposite the left toe. The stance will be more open and the feet just wide enough to give you a solid foundation – the narrower the stance, the steeper the angle of attack into the ball and the more will be the tendency for the ball to go upwards rather than forwards.

With the open stance and the ball forward, the natural path of the swing will be from out to in – outside the line on the way back, coming back to the inside on the follow-through. This, of course, is very similar to the normal bunker shot and slicing under the ball, with an open face, contributes to getting the ball up quickly, with little forward momentum on the ball.

When you've got the hang of this shot, you will feel that the harder you hit the ball, the more up in the air it will go – not further forward. This feeling in itself is a great confidence booster and will help you to avoid quitting on the shot.

Once you've mastered this, there is a further refinement for those really awkward occasions when the ground slopes away from you, the putting surface is firm and you desperately need the ball to land softly. The set-up is the same as before, but this time the swing is long, smooth and slow, and it can best be described as allowing the weight of the club to dictate the speed of the shot. It is almost as if the clubhead is swinging *you*, not the other way round. The secret is to grip the club very lightly and, at all costs, keep any tension out of the shot. Naturally this can only be attempted when one is full of confidence and off a reasonably good lie. In fact the way to gain confidence with this very difficult shot, is always to practise from a good lie with a nice carpet of grass under the ball.

Opposite: *The shot so many seem to dread! As long as there is some grass under the ball, it can be played like a straightforward bunker shot – open stance, outside-to-in swing path and the feeling of hitting the ball up, not forward. Again, grip down the shaft for greater control*

The chip

I believe that many people approach this shot without a clear idea of what it is that they are trying to do. They will use some semi-lofted club, knowing that the ball will travel partially through the air and partially along the ground. Above all, they give nowhere near the attention to the contours of the green that they would for a putt, even though the ball is going to be affected in much the same way.

I have one golden rule, which makes me think clearly and positively about how I'm going to play a chip shot. My game plan is to take a club with the right amount of loft to drop the ball just on the edge of the putting surface and then roll the rest of the way to the hole. This way I play each chip shot the same way, regardless of how far it is, or whether it is uphill or downhill. The only thing that changes is the club with which I do it.

With nothing to go over, take just enough club to carry the ball to the putting surface

Again the guiding principle with these shots is to be comfortable and balanced. As they are much shorter and there is virtually no body movement, I address the ball with the feet close together and a slightly open stance. This way I am able to look down the line of the shot and at the same time rest my right forearm against my hip – a useful thing to be able to do when you've got to get down in two to win a tournament and everything is shaking!

At the address, the hands will be a little forward of the club head and they will stay in that position throughout the shot. One thing it is important to watch out for, with the hands being forward, is that the left-hand grip doesn't become too strong – too many knuckles of the left hand showing. In this case the wrists break quickly on the take-away, and there is a tendency to drive the ball, with a loss of control over how far it goes. The shot itself is played fairly stiff-wristed, with the arms and shoulders doing most of the work.

That's the method. Thereafter there really is no substitute for some hard work around the practice green to work out which club to use in any given situation. This way you will come up to each chip shot with a simple, positive plan. Select the right club to carry the ball just onto the putting surface, so that it will roll up to the hole. It will then be relatively easy to have a clear picture in your mind of what you want the ball to do, the first prerequisite of making a good shot.

The bunker shot

For many, many golfers, a bunker is a snake-filled pit, lit by the fires of hell. It produces a dread only surpassed by having to address the ball during a fit of the shanks. Once again it is a case of understanding the demands of bunker play and having a game plan to cope with them. Then go out of a summer's evening with a few balls and get the feel of doing it correctly. So often, coming to terms with the various pieces of the short game is just a case of finding out what a good shot feels like and then working to reproduce it every time.

In many ways the normal bunker shot gives you more margin for error than most other shots. What is unfamiliar and therefore uncomfortable about it, is that it is the only shot where you positively have to hit the ground before the ball. That said, the amount of sand taken can vary and still produce a reasonable shot. Any variance in a normal shot, however, and a fluff or a thin is the result.

As with all other shots, it is necessary to have an understanding of what should happen with a bunker shot and then have a simple plan to deal with it. Once again, your mind must be filled with the picture of how the shot will look as it flies out of the sand and this will leave no room for the negative, knee-knocking thoughts that can only destroy.

The execution of the bunker shot is in many ways similar to the way you would play a short pitch. The feeling you are seeking is that the clubhead is sliding under the ball and the main force is sending the ball upwards not driving it forwards.

In the case of the greenside bunker, the wriggling of the feet into the sand is to get them below the level of the ball, so that you can still make a normal swing at the ball and the club will pass underneath, throwing it out on a cushion of sand. Since you want to enter the sand an inch or two behind the ball, set it somewhat forward in your stance, opposite the left toe. As with

The classic position for the straightforward bunker shot – feet well dug in and the ball well forward

The ball really does come out on a cushion of sand!

a chip, the stance is a little bit open, but make sure that the clubface is square to the flag. Make sure, too, that the grip is the same as for any normal shot and above all, try and avoid the fear of the shot making you grip too tightly, particularly with the left hand. This causes the strong left hand grip, with too many knuckles showing and leads to a narrow swing, a lack of rhythm and with it the tendency to dig down into the sand.

You are now set up to play from the sand. As with all short shots, it is important to get a smooth, easy rhythm. One of the best ways of getting this is to watch the best players doing it, either in the flesh or on television, and keep a mental picture of their rhythm. What with that and the picture of how the ball will come out, there really shouldn't be any room for doubts to creep in!

There is one final ingredient to ensure a good shot. Remember your feet are already the required couple of inches below the level of the ball. Consequently, there is no need for you to bend the knees into the shot. Above all, maintain a constant height throughout. Anxiety can easily make you dip or come up early, so work hard to stay still – another positive thought.

Finally, the swing itself. Unless you are a real expert, you are unlikely to be getting much backspin out of bunkers, so don't look for it. As a rough guide, a shot from a greenside bunker will roll about half the distance it has flown through the air. Try and aim, therefore, to get the ball to land about two-thirds of the way to the hole. If, through practice, you are able to get a consistent result from sand, this will become easier than you think.

One final tip that worked for me when I was growing up. For years I never had a sand wedge and always used a 9-iron from greenside bunkers. For this to work, and bearing in mind that a 9-iron does not have the thick flange of a sand wedge, it is necessary to develop a very shallow shot, with the clubhead passing only just under the ball. When I finally got the proper club, I found bunker shots really easy. In the same way that practising putting to a smaller than normal hole will make the real thing seem as big as a bucket, practising with a 9-iron from sand could improve your bunker play.

The above applies to the straightforward bunker shot from a flat lie. There are, of course, a number of more difficult situations you can find in sand, so let's deal with them.

The plugged ball

The sight of this in a bunker fills most people with alarm and despondency but, courtesy of the sand wedge, there are very few occasions when a golf ball cannot be extracted from such a lie. The natural inclination is to open the face of the club even more than usual and really heave at the ball, trying to dig it out with lots of sand. Wrong!

In fact, you go about it in a completely different way. Address the ball with it in the middle of the feet, just as though you were planning to hit a low shot into the wind. Keep the club face square to the target, which will make it hooded and in a shut position. You, yourself, are square to the target, not open.

With the ball set back in the stance, the club will come straight up from the ball and the angle of attack will be steep. You still come into the sand behind the ball, but closer than for a normal sand shot. The clubhead should drive straight down into the sand and the ball will pop up and out more easily than you might expect.

Only by experimenting, will you discover how hard the ball must be hit, but one thing is certain. There is no way that backspin can ever be imparted under these circumstances. The art is to get the ball just to pop out over the lip of the bunker, and the force required to get it out in the first place will usually be more than sufficient to get it to the pin. The secret of getting it

There's no way of getting backspin from here, but the hooded blade and the ball back in the stance makes it easier to extract than you think

to come out with as little forward momentum as possible is to grip the club very gently. As the club hits the sand, the club face opens slightly and the ball pops out more softly and slowly. As you might expect, this needs a lot of practice to perfect and there will be many occasions to start with when the ball will just flop forward a yard or two.

One of the important things in golf is to know what is and isn't possible and live with the consequence. If, in this situation, the pin is at all close to the offending bunker, there is no way of getting the ball close, short of hitting the pin. Just make certain of getting the ball out somewhere on the green, so that you only take two more to get down – limit the damage.

The poached egg

Similar to the plugged ball, but instead of being buried tight in the sand, the ball lies in a crater made by its arrival in the bunker. This type of lie only occurs in the fine, light sand you often find on links courses.

The ball can be extracted in the same way as the plugged ball, but with the sand so fine, it is difficult not to drive it out too hard. Here again, the light grip and the turning clubhead are invaluable weapons to tackle the situation.

For all bunker shots, however, it is essential to overcome irrational fear of the shot, establish a slow easy rhythm and keep tension at bay. The grip is where tension starts. Keep it firm, but not tight and above all make a complete swing at the ball, ensuring a full follow-through and do not stop the club in the sand.

Greenside trouble

Most of the foregoing deals with straightforward situations encountered day-to-day around the green, though most of you would hope that buried balls in bunkers would not be an everyday occurrence! As the wayward tee shot usually finds trouble, so the crooked approach can land you in some very awkward places.

In Britain, the design and evolution of golf courses has meant that penalties for missing greens can be severe indeed. Particularly inland, where space is often restricted, trees, bushes and out-of-bounds are sometimes menacingly close to the prepared surface. That is why you will sometimes hear professionals shout at their ball in mid-air 'Go in the sand', preferring the known and consistent problems of the bunker to the unknown and potentially expensive terrors of the surrounding areas.

Rough near the green

Whether it be long, lush grass or wiry heather, the problems posed by finding your ball in such trouble around the green can be intimidating. Further back down the hole, it's just a case of deciding what is possible and not attempting too much and so failing to get out. Close to the putting surface, it's making up your mind just how the ball will come out, given a certain strength of hit. The only known element is that it will be impossible to put any backspin on the ball or exercise much, if any, control over its behaviour. The reason for this is that, from rough, you cannot hit the ball without either the grass or the heather coming between the clubface and the ball.

Once again, it is vital to have a clear picture of the shot you intend to make. It is easy to be intimidated by difficulties confronting you and mentally surrender before the shot is hit. Accept that there won't be any stop on the ball and allow accordingly. Above all, make certain, if at all possible, that you get back onto the putting surface first time. It may mean that you don't actually play directly for the pin, but a long putt is preferable to the embarrassment of having to hit a second pitch or chip, having been too ambitious with the first.

As for the shot itself, the most effective method, nine times out of ten, is to play it like a bunker shot – open stance, clubface open, long, easy swing from out-to-in across the line and throw the ball high in the air, with as little forward momentum as possible. There's no guarantee that it will flop out close to the pin, but it takes away the mental picture of the green as a runway, with the ball a plane going too fast to stop before it crashes off the end.

If you get the chance, take a few balls one evening and try the shot out near one of the greens on your course. Once you get the hang of it, you will see how it increases the margin of error. In fact, it makes the green a bigger target, with the ball dropping gently onto it, rather than driven low and hard as is otherwise the case. Watch out for the head greenkeeper, though!

Bare and muddy lies

This is one area of golf where we professionals are more fortunate than most club golfers, particularly in this country. We tend to play all our golf on courses specially prepared for major events and, of course, the tournament circuit always follows the sun. Even so, with our recent, rainy summers, conditions are often far from ideal, but then there are always the tournament officials with their cans of white spray to ring off any offending area. So, all in all, we have very little to complain of by way of unsatisfactory conditions, particularly round greens.

Not so the club golfer, especially if he is a hardy soul, and always there for the Sunday fourball, unless the course is under a foot of snow. For him, the bare, worn lie – bone hard in summer and muddy in winter – can be an occasional feature.

Many golfers like to use a sand-iron for pitching to greens, certainly when there is an obstacle to go over. This is fine if there is a reasonable depth of grass under the ball, but fatal if the lie is bare. The very shape of the sole of a sand-iron means that the leading edge sits up off the ground and a fluff or thin is the almost certain result if you attempt to nip the ball off a bare lie. If you need loft, use a pitching wedge or 9-iron. If not, the straighter-faced a club you use the better. In fact don't be ashamed of the putter, if there's no obstacle between you and the green and the approach area is reasonably flat. Remember, the first objective is to get the ball on the putting surface.

Again, it is most important to have a clear picture of the type of shot you are trying, and keep all those negative thoughts at bay. The ball should be quite well back in the stance and the hands ahead of the clubhead throughout the shot. Above all, visualize a nice, clean, crisp stroke.

5 Putting: The Game within the Game

If Mr Average Golfer spends too much time tinkering with his long game at the expense of the short, his neglect of his putting skills verges on the criminal. Whatever your standard, you will use the putter more than twice as much as any other club in your bag and if you are a really good player, say scratch to 5 handicap, it will account for nearly 50 per cent of the shots hit in a round. Yet how often is the putting green at your club full of members working on this part of their game?

On the pro tour, unless you are averaging 31, or at most, 32 putts a round, then you will spend your life in a caravan. And 31 or 32 putts is only acceptable if you are hitting virtually every green in regulation. In years gone by, great strikers not only survived in professional golf with a poor putting stroke, but sometimes even won tournaments. Today, I cannot think of a bad putter on the Tour, and most can go on holing those testing 5-footers over the closing holes, when it really matters.

With so many more tournaments now and the opportunity to compete somewhere in the world whenever you want to, the top professionals are permanently being faced with putts worth many thousands of pounds. So much so, that even the downhill 4-footer for £20,000 is becoming commonplace and, dare I say it, less frightening.

Every year, more and more golfers are making spectacular livings out of the game, such is the dramatic increase in prize money almost everywhere and long may it continue. Nick Faldo recently explained how little pressure he felt playing tournament golf, as he now had all the money he could possibly want. That left him free to concentrate on the one thing he really wanted, which was to win titles. This is getting to be true of most of those who regularly occupy the top spots in tour events and so the pressure on that final putt gets less and less. That said, the man who says his knees aren't shaking as he stands there with 'this to win', is lying!

The mental image

I've mentioned before the importance of having a clear mental picture of the shot you are about to hit. This is even more true in putting. You must pick the line you truly believe will take the ball into the hole and then retain the vision of the ball rolling along that line and into the cup. Only this way will you make a positive stroke at the ball and hit it at the right pace to do the job.

Every line selection is based on two factors: the slope of the green and how hard you intend to hit the ball. If the ball is going to die into the hole then it will take more borrow than if it still has a foot or so to run as it pops in. The slope of the green is fairly easy to read to make the necessary adjustments to right or left.

The pace is down to you and this is where the mental picture of the ball running into the hole is so important as that will have a great influence on how hard you hit it. If you are having to think about the strength of a putt, you are unlikely to make a decisive or positive stroke. So, time spent practising putting is vital. Not only will you hopefully be perfecting a stroke that sends the ball in the direction you want, but you will also be building in an awareness of distance which will enable you to judge pace without having to think about it.

Of course you also have to believe you do have a putting stroke that sends the ball where you want. Putting is a very personal and individual thing. More than in any other part of the game, there are a myriad of methods – and implements – for getting the ball into the hole. There are, however, a number of basic ingredients that are essential to being a consistently good putter.

The putting stroke

Throughout my life, I have tried to make the golf swing I've got work. I've never tried to change it to something that might, or might not, be more effective. That is perhaps the reason I appear to have one of the more natural swings amongst the top golfers. A constant theme of mine to achieve this is, as I have said elsewhere, to change as little as possible from one type of shot to the next. I carry this right through to the putter as well.

Certainly one of the important factors in my great year of 1987 was an improvement in my putting and, in the main, I put this down to lengthening the shaft an inch or so. Being on the short side, I stand more upright than

My putting stance – upright and slightly open, similar to my natural address position for the whole of my game

Jack Nicklaus, a great experimenter with different methods, and putters, in his most familiar pose – feet close together and the ball well forward in the stance

most to hit the golf ball. Lengthening the shaft enabled me to carry this through to the putting stroke as well and it immediately felt more comfortable, more natural.

In hitting a golf ball, my stance is, if anything, slightly open. The same is true when putting. In fact my whole address position is almost an exact replica of when I'm chipping – right elbow on hip, head slightly behind the ball, looking down the line, hands just in front of the clubhead.

When tinkering about, as one always does when looking for improvements in the short game, I discovered early on that the wider the stance, within reason, the flatter the putting stroke. This is desirable, as any descending blow increases the chances of hitting the ball into the green rather than along it. All photographic evidence shows that every putt hops a bit before it starts rolling along the green. Consistency of direction as well as distance are improved the quicker you can get it rolling.

Look at most of the top golfers and you will notice that they putt with their feet apart. One exception, and then only at certain times of his career, is Jack Nicklaus. It would have been impossible to have done what he has without being a very good putter, but if there has been any part of his game that has not been in a class above the rest of the world, it is on the greens. That said, when he does putt with his feet close together, he positions the ball opposite or even ahead of the left foot and so is still able to achieve a shallow angle of attack into the ball.

The putting stroke itself has changed significantly over the years. In the first half of this century, nearly everyone used the wrists as hinges, keeping the rest of the body motionless. The belief was, the less moving parts there were, the less could go wrong at moments of extreme stress.

If anyone changed this view, it must have been Bob Charles, who for more than ten years in the late fifties and sixties was probably the best putter the world has ever seen. He carried the theory to its logical conclusion and kept everything locked rigid, moving the clubhead backwards and forwards with his shoulders.

Between these two extreme methods have evolved most of today's putting techniques, with a light loosening of the wrists on the backswing, but the hands staying ahead of the putter throughout the stroke and quite a lot of movement with the shoulders and arms. Certainly more Bob Charles than, say, Billy Casper or Arnold Palmer.

I certainly fall within this category, believing, as do most, that this is the best way of keeping the blade of the putter square to the hole throughout the stroke. The feeling is that wristy putters may occasionally have spectacu-

The wristy putting stroke of Billy Casper (left) versus the rigid method of Bob Charles

lar days on the greens, but consistency is far harder to achieve, both in judgment of distance and in hitting the ball on the line selected.

Of greatest importance, though, is that our type of putting stroke is logically the best. Belief is a great aid to underpinning one's confidence and it's confidence that really matters when the crunch comes. We believe that if you can keep the blade square throughout the stroke, then one of the variables has been removed from the equation. Thereafter, you only have to pick the right line and get the strength right. What could be easier!

The Grip

Though I have just said that the putting stroke is a miniature of my full golf swing, certainly in stance and set-up, the grip is completely different. I like to feel that the palm of my right hand is facing the hole and opposite to my left palm, so that the back of that hand is aimed directly at the hole. Like most other players, I also change my normal Vardon grip (little finger of the right hand overlapping the left forefinger) to the reverse overlap – left forefinger over right little finger. This has two advantages. The hands are still moulded together and continue to work as a single unit and it also tightens the tendons of the left wrist, which helps keep that wrist firm throughout the putting stroke.

My putting grip, back of the left hand and the palm of the right towards the hole

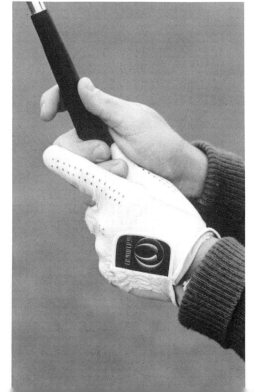
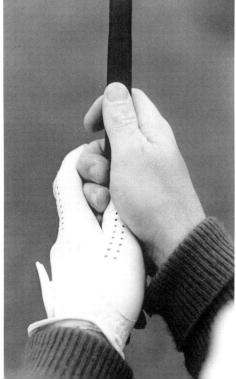

These are the basic ingredients, though the minor details change from time to time. For example, on really quick greens, where a very gentle stroke is required, I might go down the grip for greater clubhead control. Or, if I'm not holing as many putts as I feel I should, I sometimes experiment with leaving the right forefinger almost off the shaft like Ballesteros, or with the left forefinger down the knuckles of the right hand rather than overlapping the little finger, the way that Mark McNulty does.

One final check on the hardware that you use. The thickness of the grip should be just right for the size and shape of your hands. It is often said that so-and-so has a very delicate touch on the greens 'for such a big man'. Why shouldn't a large man putt as well as a little one? One very good reason is that, if his hands are in proportion to the rest of his body, he will require a much thicker grip on his putter than the rest of us. The thicker the grip, the harder it is to 'feel' the clubhead and so have the sensitivity to putt very well.

If the grip of the putter is too thin for your hands, it can make it difficult to grip correctly – think how hard it would be to hold the putter, if you just had the shaft to hang on to. Too thick, and the weapon becomes very clumsy. Imagine putting with a cricket bat.

Last but not least, the condition of the grip of the putter is just as important as with the rest of the clubs in the bag. Many people still have leather grips on their putters and if these get shiny, the natural instinct is to hang on tighter, as they feel the club might slip around. This may not be a conscious feeling, but it can totally destroy the touch and the tempo of the putting stroke and a golfer might be totally unaware of the cause.

Grip pressure

This last comment brings me to the vital question of how hard to grip the club when putting. The answer is – as lightly as possible. Two of the great experts on the greens, Ballesteros and Bobby Locke, have both said that they hold the club so gently that it almost falls out of their hands. No one would argue that it is on the greens that they feel the most pressure and tension and I have seen many club golfers almost strangling the club, as a result of that tension.

If your grip is too tight, whatever the reason, it will create rigidity and tension in the rest of your body and it will be much harder to make a smooth stroke at the ball. Remember, a putt is a caress of the ball, not an uninhibited bash.

One of the reasons for gripping tightly is, I suspect, concern about twitching on the greens. The feeling is, grip firmly and everything will be that much more under control. The reverse is true and if you are having a jerky time on the greens, just check that you are not hanging on for dear life.

Whilst on the unattractive subject of the twitch, many of you will know that one of the popular solutions is to swap the hands around, putting the left below right. The thinking, and it's quite correct, is that this prevents the right hand involuntarily taking over and shoving the head of the putter ahead of the hands and wrists. Again, the grip should be light.

Ball position

With putting being such a personal exercise, where the ball should be in relation to the feet is very much up to the individual concerned. Some people putt with the ball almost touching the toes, others with the ball so far away you feel they must fall over to reach it. Again, the choice of where in the stance the ball should be positioned can vary all the way from outside the left foot to opposite the right.

Neil Coles is someone who has always had the ball so close to his left toe that I sometimes wonder if he has ever hit his foot. His consistency and the fact that he is still able to hold his own on the European Tour after more than 30 years at the top, is proof that what he does works. At the other extreme, Ben Crenshaw, who many believe has been the best putter in the world during the last decade, seems to me to be uncomfortably far away from the ball. But his pendulum stroke keeps the ball rolling smoothly into the hole.

Many of you will remember the way he kept holing out against Eamonn Darcy in that vital Ryder Cup singles in America with a 2- or 3-iron, having broken his faithful putter earlier in the round. I believe that only someone so used to having the ball a long way from the body could have performed so well on such an occasion, having lost the most vital club in the bag. In the end it was actually his long game that let him down and enabled Eamonn to catch him on the last green.

In line with my creed of being comfortable when setting up for all shots and changing as little as possible throughout my game, I usually place the ball forward in the stance, just inside the left foot and just far enough away so that when I take up my stance I have got my head over the ball. I have mentioned about width of stance and, with the ball fairly well forward, this enables me to have a nice low stroke, both back and through the ball. That

Neil Coles (left) *always looks as if he is going to hit his left toe, so close does he stand to the ball*

Crenshaw (right) *putted brilliantly with a long iron in the 1987 Ryder Cup*

Above: *Under more normal circumstances, Crenshaw is still one of the great putters of the world*

Below: *There is no correct way to stand to a putt and, in my case, small changes are introduced from time to time. Note the different stance and ball position in these two pictures taken some months apart during the 1988 season*

said, in 1988, I moved the ball back a little in my stance and found that worked for most of the year – all part of the continual tinkering that keeps the short game fresh and in tune. However, beware of change for change's sake.

Putting is something that needs constant attention, both to preserve what's right as well as to seek improvements. It is very easy for bad habits to creep in and before trying something different check that nothing has changed to make you putt badly. It is much better to find your old method and rhythm, than to adopt a new set of procedures which will take a long time to groove and inspire confidence.

Good striking

Every golfer knows the joy of the shot that goes 'right off the button'. He or she will also know that the well-struck shot goes that much further than one off the toe or the heel or some other unmentionable part of the club. To a much less obvious degree, the same is true of a putt.

How often have you heard an opponent say, having left an approach putt a yard short of the hole, 'I didn't hit it hard enough', when the reality is that he probably didn't strike it properly? Not finding the 'sweet spot' on the putter blade can perhaps mean the difference of one yard on a 25-yard putt. Judgment of distance is difficult enough, without building in an extra variant of your own creation.

As well as the importance of finding the right spot on the club face every time, the actual way you strike the ball affects how far it travels. Earlier I mentioned how keeping the clubhead low to the ground throughout the putting stroke contributed to getting the ball rolling more quickly. The better you do this, the less strength will be needed to get the ball up to the hole.

So, to gain consistency when judging distance on putts, it is important to find both the right part of the clubface with which to hit the ball, and to strike the ball in such a way as to get it rolling along the green smoothly. Here are a couple of tips to make this easier to do.

First, establish exactly where on the clubface the sweet spot is. You can do this by taking one of the harder balls on the market and bouncing it on the face of the putter. The sweet spot will produce a deeper, more hollow note than the rest of the blade. Having found the spot, mark it with a crayon or similar and practise hitting the ball with that spot on the putting green.

Secondly, concentrate on hitting a precise point on the ball, not just the whole thing. You may wonder why so many of the tournament pros continu-

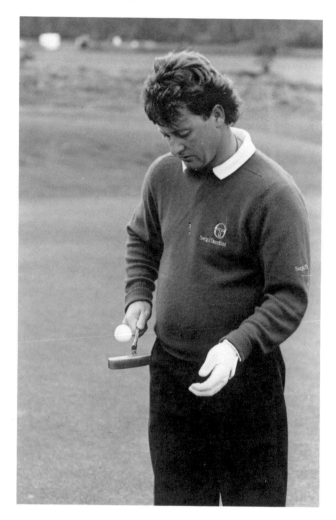

Finding the sweet spot

ally pick the ball up and mark it, sometimes from very close range. One of the prime reasons is to replace the ball in such a way that some of the lettering will be at the exact spot where the putter should strike the ball. They then consciously aim at that spot.

All this may sound a bit detailed, but it is an essential part of trying to eliminate some of the variables from that area of the game where shots can be saved, or indeed wasted, more easily than anywhere else. Perhaps its greatest benefit, though, is that it gives the player positive things to concentrate on and helps stop the mind filling up with those negative thoughts about all the things that might go wrong.

Picking the right line

Most of the time it is fairly easy to see which way the green slopes and therefore which side of the hole to aim at. The skill is in judging how much to borrow. The more golf you play and, hopefully, the better you become, the more instinctive this judgment becomes.

However, the amount you allow will depend on how hard you intend to hit the ball, as well as the degree of slope on the green. For example, downhill

Hubert Green plumb-bobbing – though it helps to have a straight putter shaft!

on a fairly quick green, only an ounce too much strength means the ball will be 5 feet past. Hoping to get the pace exactly right will mean that the putt will use all of the borrow that exists. Uphill, on a slow green, with no fear of going a long way by, you can strike firmly for the hole and the ball will not have reacted much to the slope of the green before it disappears into the cup. Certainly, the quicker the putting surface, the more the ball will react to whatever slopes there are.

On many of the older courses, particularly at the seaside, the crumpled, natural contours mean that you will often have a putt that, say, goes right to start with, only to move back left as it gets nearer the hole. Taking the point that the slower the ball is travelling, the more borrow it will take, then the slope of the ground around the hole will have much more effect than the lie of the land from where the putt is struck.

It's in circumstances like this, where the correct line is difficult to read, that the art of 'plumb-bobbing' comes into play. Plumb-bobbing is where the golfer stands behind the ball, directly in line with the hole and holds his putter up vertically. Closing one eye, he will line the bottom of the shaft through the centre of the ball and looking further up the shaft he will see that the hole is either to the right or left of it. Whichever side the shaft is, that is the side to aim the putt and the further the top of the shaft is away from the hole, the more borrow the ball will take.

One further point, and perhaps the most important aspect of line selection. Having decided which side to aim and by how much, pick a specific spot to aim *at*. Imagine that every putt is a straight putt. Only the contours of the green will move it one way or the other. Unless you are aware of this, you are inclined to stand open on left-to-right putts and closed on right-to-left ones. This will cause you to cut, or slice, putts from the left and hook those from the other side. Always pick your spot and make a straight putt of it.

Choosing the right putter

Finding the perfect putter has been the eternal search of all golfing mankind. The belief that it's the weapon not the man has kept the club professionals in funds, if not actually in riches, ever since the game began. Over the years though, those with the reputation of being the best at getting the ball into the hole have usually found the putter of their dreams early on and stuck with it through thick and thin – more thick than thin, when it comes to their bank balances!

Bobby Locke with his Gem, Seve with his Ping and Ben Crenshaw with his Wilson blade – it's impossible to think of them with anything else in their hands on the putting green. They have all reached that blissful state where they just know they have the one club that is absolutely right for them. Good putting is, amongst other things, the banishment of doubt. For them, in the area of the right tool for the job, there are no doubts.

For the rest, the endless hunt for the right weapon, as well as the perfect method or, at least, the momentary gimmick, will continue. And after all, that's half the fun. There are, however, one or two pointers that can perhaps narrow the search for you in the future.

I mentioned earlier the importance of finding the sweet spot on a putter and learning to hit the ball from it all the time. On different types of putter, the sweet spot is in different places. What is also true, is that on some putters the sweet spot is wider than on others. In simple terms, as the putter has evolved over the years, the sweet spot has got wider.

When the game of golf began, the putter was just a shorter, more upright, straight-faced version of any other golf club. Perhaps the best example was the Calamity Jane used by Bobby Jones. The modern equivalent is Ben Crenshaw's Wilson. On these types of putters, where the whole of the blade is one side of the shaft, the sweet spot is comparatively small.

Not long after the turn of the century, the first centre-shafted putter was invented. Known then, or soon after, as the Schenectady, it went through various stages of evolution until, after the last war, the most famous version of all was produced – the Bullseye, manufactured by the Acushnet Company of America. In this country, its equivalent was the Golden Goose. Today, very few of the top players use one of these, though Greg Norman has one as an alternative to his blade putter. Just extending the blade behind the point where the shaft joins it increases the sweet spot and its greatest appeal has been that it enables people to strike the ball very close to the bottom of the shaft.

Mr Karsten and his Ping made the biggest breakthrough at the beginning of the 1960s. The real winning feature of his putter was that the weight was situated at the heel and toe of the blade, thus dramatically increasing the area from which you could get a perfect strike. Early on, he became aware that golfers didn't need the audible evidence of a correct strike and the disconcerting sound, which gave the early models their name, was removed.

You may think that the width of sweet spot is not important, but without constant practice, the area of the blade which comes into contact with the

Bobby Locke and his 'Gem' – with the sales he achieved for this type of putter, just imagine what his endorsement contract would have been today!

ball some time during the round is surprisingly large. Just by being aware that this is the case will probably help you strike your putts better and with more consistency.

As I have mentioned before, it is vital to be comfortable on all golf shots. If you have been playing golf for several years, you will probably have found a stance and a position for putting with which you are happy. Your putter must have the right length of shaft and the right shaft/blade angle to suit your posture.

It would be easy to say that the taller you are, the longer should be the shaft, but there are many variables. Straight arms or bent elbows can alter the length of shaft by several inches. Some people stand up straight, others

The long and the short of it: the contrasting styles of Ray Floyd (left) *and Andy North, two men of similar height*

like to bend right over. Andy North and Ray Floyd are about the same height, but North must have his hands 2 feet nearer the ground than Floyd when putting. And remember, don't just chop a few inches off your existing putter if you feel you want a shorter one – it will completely alter the balance. The same is true when lengthening a club. It can be done, but be aware that other factors will change as well.

A desirable feature of your stance should be that the head, or more precisely the eyes, be right over the top of the ball. This not only ensures that you look straight down the line of the putt when you look at the hole but, with the top half of your body more over the ball, it is easier to keep the blade of the putter square to the hole throughout the stroke.

Thereafter, it is up to you how far you like to have your hands away from the body and this in turn will decide the angle of the shaft to the putter blade.

The eyes should be right over the top of the ball – a little room for improvement here!

105

Practising

As with every aspect of the game, putting must be done with a specific purpose in mind and within a framework designed to produce results. Not only will the aimless striking of putts be valueless, it can be positively damaging, particularly if you start experimenting with an area of your game that is working satisfactorily.

With putting, practice should be designed either for getting the ball in the hole more often from short range, or improving judgment of distance from long range. Therefore all my practice is done from less than 10 feet or more than 30 feet. Finally, I concentrate on one or other aspect per session, very rarely mixing them up.

Short putts

From close range, practice is all about building confidence in your ability to put the ball in the hole. It stands to reason that the more often you physically achieve this, the greater will be the belief in your own ability.

The secret is to start close to the hole, about 3 feet away, with perhaps three balls and only move back a foot at a time when all three have gone in. Every time you miss one, back to the beginning and start again from 3 feet. It will only take a putt or two to work out the correct line, so this is an exercise in perfecting your ability to hit the ball along a decreed route.

It also brings an important element of personal competition into practice by seeing how far away from the hole you can get without missing a putt. The build-up of pressure, the further away from the hole you get, is excellent preparation for those testing short ones in medal or match play.

Most people would say that their favourite short putt (if there is such a thing) would be a straight one, slightly uphill, or perhaps with a touch of right-to-left borrow. Conversely, the most loathed is the down-hiller, left-to-right. In competition, it's no good coming up to 'one of those', knowing you hate it and with your mind full of mental pictures of Doug Sanders on the 18th green at St Andrews in the 1970 Open Championship.

To combat this, and to approach all short putts from whatever angle positively, I find a hole on a gentle slope and arrange eight or nine balls in a circle around it, again starting close in. In knocking those balls into the hole, you will be faced with all varieties of short putt – uphill, downhill, right-to-left and left-to-right. Every time you complete the circle, you set it up further away, only returning to the original distance every time you fail to hole one. Always remember that your ultimate aim is to hole a sequence of putts from about 10 feet, so these personal competitions are winnable!

Long putts

Practising these is all about building confidence in your ability to judge distance perfectly on whatever greens you may encounter. You are not concerned about the number of times you can get the ball in the hole from long range; rather you are seeking consistency in hitting the ball a required distance.

Once again, take three balls and concentrate solely on getting them level with whatever target you are aiming at. Finding the right line is much the easier of the two elements of getting a long putt close to the hole, and your first practice putt will give you the line anyway.

It is easy to get loose and sloppy on long putts, with too long a backswing and too short a follow-through. Try and make your long putting stroke equidistant either side of the ball – 6 inches back, 6 inches through and so on.

Long-distance putting is also about finding that elusive sweet spot on the putter blade more often. So when practising, listen and feel for that right spot on the club face. An aid to this, having found the spot, is the method I have already suggested: to mark it with a piece of crayon or chalk both on the club face and on the top of the blade. If necessary, you can make the mark on the top of the blade permanent if you are happy with it.

Finally, it is impossible to judge distance correctly if you are not delivering the blade square to the ball every time – in fact, you won't hole the short ones either. So take your three balls and paint a line round the middle of each one. Line each ball up with the stripe pointing in the direction you intend to putt. If you are striking the ball correctly, it will role to the target along the painted line. Only as it begins to lose speed and take the borrow, should the line begin to wobble.

Competition

The finest way of sharpening your competitive edge on the greens is to putt against someone else for money. There is nothing to beat the simulation of a match environment to prepare you for the real thing. On your club practice putting green, the more often you go round, the more certain you will become of the line. So, if you regularly play someone for a few bob, you will soon discover how good you are at hitting a putt on the right line, at the right speed as the pressure mounts.

The trouble with most practice greens is that they usually consist of 9 or 18 holes all measuring in the 12 to 20 feet range; putts you don't really expect to hole, but nice if they fall in, and of course you are very unlikely to three-putt. It is also a distance you don't often leave yourself in real competition. If you hit the green in the right number of shots, you will probably end up further away, and if you are pitching or chipping you should be getting closer.

Many other practice greens just have long putts of 25 or 30 feet and above, and going round those is just a game of who can three-putt the least. Far better then to design your own course, making it a mixture of 3- to 10-footers, intermingled with a number of 30-foot plus putts.

There are a variety of formats for introducing a competitive element into putting against chums – straight matches, accumulators etc. When playing in Ryder Cups and the like, we have a couple of favourite variations.

First we play two balls each and have aggregate competitions. If you are much over level 3s for your two balls, it usually costs you money! Secondly, and this can be really vicious, we play a version of putter lengths. This is not the usual concession of any putt shorter than the length of shaft below the grip. In our game, having putted at the hole and missed, we have to lay the putter down behind the ball, away from the hole, and play the second putt from where the ball originally came to rest PLUS the length of the putter. In other words, you always move the ball some 3 feet further away each time. Using a medal format and at $5 per shot, it can be a very exciting, not to say expensive, game!

So you see, there are all sorts of ways of using your time on the practice green that are both beneficial and enjoyable, and even rewarding. Just make certain that when you go out there you know what it is you are trying to achieve, even if it is only to inflict financial ruin on your best friend!

6 The Brain Game

In the earlier chapters, I hope I have given a reasonably clear and simple picture of how I hit the ball, what I think is important in a golf swing and a few hints as to how to improve your striking in a variety of situations.

What most amateurs have to recognize is that, once into a working career and later into family life, there will be limitations on how much time can be devoted to the game of golf. All too many people waste that precious time trying to change their basic method in the hopeless pursuit of the perfect swing. Swings can be changed, but you only have to witness the titanic struggles of Nick Faldo during the four years it took him to complete *his* alterations to begin to appreciate the time, commitment and effort required. So much better to spend what little time you have making the most of what you've got.

Any reasonably competent golfer, say with a handicap of less than 18, would probably admit to being happy with the quality of strike he achieves with his best shot. He therefore already has the ability to do it. All he wants to do is produce it more often.

Close attention to, and constant checking of, the fundamentals of the game – grip, stance, ball position, head still, balance and rhythm – will produce far more consistency and do more for quality of shot than most amateur golfers would ever imagine. It is variation in these, rather than changing swings, that produce the ups and downs in the everyday life of the ordinary golfer. Pay attention to them and service them regularly and you will be surprised how much more consistent you are. So back to the earlier chapters and see that you have got them right.

Continuing this theme of seeing that you have got the engine of your game running as smoothly as possible, there are a number of other areas often neglected or not even thought about, that can greatly influence how well you play from day to day.

Equipment

Were you to go out and spend £500 to £1000 on a new suit, you would expect to be measured carefully for it and for there to be several fittings before finally taking delivery. Why then not adopt the same careful approach to your golf clubs? It is just as important for them to fit properly, as it is for a new suit.

As I am sure many of you are aware, I speak from experience, having spent many months working with the manufacturers of my clubs, to ensure that they are just what I need. In addition, I have spent hundreds of hours on the practice ground testing each variation and, having got what I wanted, becoming totally familiar with the final edition.

What I am saying is – 'Buy from your pro' – or at least from one who understands how to match up a golfer and his clubs. It is just possible that the clubs you have got are not really the beautifully matched set you thought them to be. Most competent club professionals have the accurate, and not particularly sophisticated, equipment to check them over and make the necessary adjustments.

What am I talking about? Well, every golf club has a number of variables; features that could make it right for one person, but unsuitable for another. The obvious ones are the weight of the club and the whippiness of the shaft. In addition there is the loft and lie of the club, the length of the shaft and the thickness of the grip. In a properly matched set, these all come together to achieve a uniform swing weight throughout the set. If your clubs aren't matching, you are introducing variables into your game, when your number one priority is to eliminate them as far as possible.

Not only is it important for you to have a truly matched set of clubs, but the features of your clubs should be right for you. It's no good being 25 years of age, 6 feet tall and weighing 14 stone and expecting to play good golf with lightweight clubs and a whippy shaft. Conversely, there's no point having an exact replica of Jack Nicklaus' clubs, if you are nearing retirement age and suffer from tennis elbow.

So let us just look at the features mentioned above, all of which must be right, if you are to maximize your ability on the course.

Weight of club

As a general principle, the bigger, younger and stronger you are, the heavier the club you can use. Up to a certain point, the heavier the club, the further

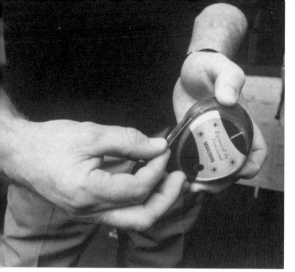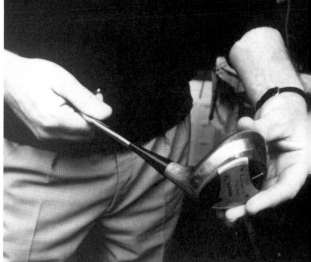

Above: *Extra weight can be experimented with, by fixing lead tape to the back of the club. . . .*

. . . and made permanent by filling the clubhead with lead (below)

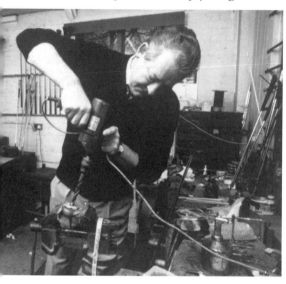

the ball will travel, provided that the clubhead speed remains constant. However, of the two, clubhead speed is the more dominant factor in determining the distance a ball flies.

The weight of a club should be such that the user can feel the head at the end of the shaft, but at all times be in control of it. There is a myth that if someone has a fast swing, getting heavier clubs will slow him down. True, but it will also result in loss of clubhead control, often with worse consequences than those produced by the fast swing. The practice ground is the

111

place to find and groove rhythm and tempo – don't try and buy it in the pro's shop.

Return to the competent club professional. He will be able to advise you on the sort of weight of club that would be right for you.

Flexibility of shaft

The more flexibility there is in a shaft, the greater is the skill and control needed to deliver the club square to the ball at impact. As a general principle, the slower the swing, the whippier the shaft can be, as the clubhead speed will come from the shaft and not from the speed of swing.

Obviously, the heavier the clubhead, the more whippiness it will induce in a given shaft. Consequently, the young and fit amongst us, whose ideal club will be heavier than that of the older and not so strong, will also require a stiffer shaft to produce the right combination of clubhead and shaft to suit his game.

As you can see the weight of the club and the whippiness of the shaft are totally interlinked and again the club professional should be able to guide you in the right direction. He will of course need to know your game, or at least see you hit a number of shots, to have an idea of what would suit you best. However, I'm sure he will give some time for free, if there is to be a set of clubs sold at the end of it. Come to think of it, he might even throw in a couple of lessons as well!

Loft and lie

To have the best chance of hitting a good shot, particularly with an iron club, the angle of the shaft to the clubhead must be right for your height and build. When you take your natural address position, the toe of the club should be just off the ground, so much so, that you could just slide a ten pence piece under it. As we are all different heights, it stands to reason that the angle of the shaft to the clubhead varies from one individual to another. The taller you are, the more acute the angle between shaft and clubhead. This is known as the lie of the club and without any contortions from you, your clubs should be set up to reflect accurately your height and stance.

The loft is the angle of the clubface to the ground and determines how high a ball flies and consequently how far it goes. In a well-matched set, each successive club has a few more degrees of loft than its predecessor and what each club should be is well documented and pre-determined.

Today, such is the skill and precision of the top manufacturers, that very few sets come out of the factory that are not well-matched – for the average golfer. This may not be right for *you*. If you are tall or short, the clubs may need adjusting, both for loft and lie. The tall man will probably need his clubs to be more upright. With his more upright swing producing a steeper angle of attack into the ball, he will tend to hit the ball higher than normal and therefore want the loft to be reduced a degree or so on each club. Lee Trevino, when he comes to this country and because he encounters windier conditions here, has the loft on his irons reduced by 1 degree, to enable him to hit the ball lower than in the States.

All these variations and adjustments can be carried out on what it unscientifically known as a 'loft and lie machine'. Many club professionals have them. Remember too, that with normal play, clubs can be knocked out of shape and should be regularly checked to see if they are still as well matched as when you bought them.

The loft and lie machine, with the loft being calibrated by the arm on the right and the lie on the left

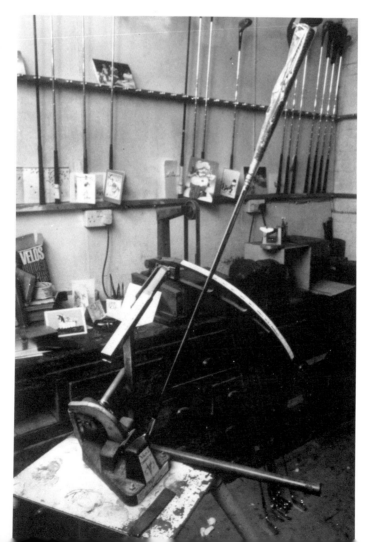

Length of shaft

Not all the necessary adjustments can be made by sticking your clubs in the vice – because that's all a 'loft and lie machine' is. If you are much taller than average, then the normal length of shaft can cause you to stoop – or push you back on your heels if you are a bit on the short side. With the help of your professional you should specify the length of shaft required.

Whilst on the issue of shaft length, it is worth noting that existing clubs can be shortened or lengthened without too much difficulty. To lengthen a club, the grip is removed and a metal shaft extender inserted in the top of the shaft to the required length. This is also one way of overcoming the excessive cost of kitting out growing children, without having to buy a new set every other year. To shorten clubs, the shaft is sawn off by the appropriate amount and then regripped.

Thickness of grips

On the theme that we are all built differently, the shape and size of our hands obviously vary enormously. This has to be accommodated by the thickness of the grips on our clubs.

The manufacturers recognize the difference between men and women and provide accordingly. For large hands though, extra thickness has to be created by tape around the shaft, underneath the grip. Make certain that your grips are the right size for you.

There are thick and thin rubber grips, but extra variations can be built in by using tape between the grip and the shaft

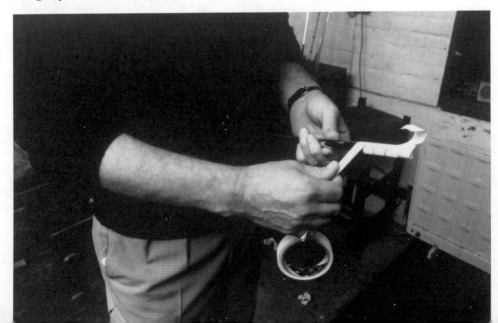

Finally, the swing weight is measured to ensure that the whole set has a matched 'feel' to it – each club feeling the same weight when swung

Most of the above applies to the purchase of new clubs, or at least as a check on what you've got, to ensure that your clubs are up to scratch and that you are not playing under some previously unsuspected handicap. But, as with any piece of machinery, your clubs need to be kept in good working order and may require occasional servicing.

I have already mentioned the checking of the loft and lie, and that should be done on an annual basis. Grips will always become worn and sometimes shiny and slippery with age. They can be made to last longer by regular scrubbing, but in the end will need renewing. A shiny grip can quickly alter the way you hold the club and induce tension by forcing you to grip more tightly than you otherwise should.

I have often heard golfers say that a certain club, say a 5- or a 6-iron, is their favourite, without being able to say why. It could be that it differs slightly from the rest in some way or other. Whatever it may be, check the others against it and make sure they match it in every way measurable.

Shafts, too, eventually 'die' and performance is impaired – it may not just be increasing age that causes you to lose length! If you have a set of clubs that you like the look and feel of, then they can easily be reshafted and with a bit of buffing and polishing, can revitalize your game for a fraction of the cost of a new set.

In talking about matched sets of clubs, I am only referring to the irons and just 1 or 2 to 9 at that. All the other clubs in the bag I regard as specials and scour the world on my travels for anything that might cut those vital shots off my score. I refer, of course, to the drivers, fairway woods, the wedges and the putters.

Look in any professional's bag and you will find very few who have matched sets of woods, or wedges that are part of their set of irons. Most people recognize the individual qualities necessary in a putter, but the same is also true of these other clubs. Keep your eyes open as you go through the pros shops in any clubs you may visit and you could find a club that really suits your game. Apart from the benefits it may bring, it's great fun just looking.

Practising

Practice should be a regular and purposeful activity, with time set aside for it out of the hours that you are able to spend at the golf club. All too often, a spell on the practice ground is something that only happens when there isn't a game about, or you don't have enough time to fit in a whole round.

Many hours are spent on the practice tee away from the public's gaze

Under these circumstances, the bag of balls is reluctantly dragged out of the car boot and 50 or 60 shots fired off aimlessly into the distance. Not only is this a waste of time, it can be positively dangerous, as, without a plan, you will often react to shots you hit out there and change something that was previously working well. In much the same way that a good shot rarely occurs without a positive mental picture of how it should work out, practice is valueless, and of little pleasure, unless you have a clear idea of what it is you are trying to achieve.

So here are some guidelines which you should use as the basis for the time you spend on the practice ground. Follow these for a few months and I would be surprised if there wasn't an improvement – in the number of victories on a Sunday morning, if not your actual handicap. I am referring now to genuine practice sessions, not the few shots you should fire off to loosen up prior to playing a round:

1. Set aside half an hour on each visit to the club to hit some shots. If the visit coincides with a game of golf, the practice session should be after the round and maybe concentrate on a part of the game that didn't go quite right.

2. Build up the number of shots you hit during the session to 50 or 60 — more than this can get boring and result in you cutting out the session next time. Set an upper limit and you will find yourself keen to get back.
3. Have a clear idea what it is you are trying to achieve and how you are going to go about it. Concentrate on one aspect of your game per session and stick to the plan throughout.
4. Always have a target to aim at and even if the practice ground lacks posts or flags, line up on a tree or chimney pot in the distance.
5. Be aware that 75 per cent of shots are hit with the medium irons or less and apportion your practice time accordingly. Chipping and putting are just as important as any part of the long game and probably offer more scope for improvement than any other aspect of your game. Above all, resist the temptation to go and hit those shots at which you know you are best. I know they are the most pleasurable, but the time is better spent elsewhere.
6. Concentrating on one aspect at a time should mean that you will be using one club, or a series of clubs, for the session. As well as having a target to aim at, work at getting consistency of distance with each club, as well as directional accuracy.
7. At all times realize that the practice ground is the place to build rhythm into your swing. Resist the natural tendency to hit harder and harder as the session goes on. It is also easy to speed up without realizing it, so restrict your strike rate to three shots per minute or less.
8. As well as trying to hit the ball straight, mix in fades and draws. Also try hitting the ball high and low. Not only does this break any monotony that may creep in; it also gives an awareness of what these shots feel like. Remember though, always use the same basic swing — no special swings are necessary.

As I said, the above suggestions refer to practice sessions designed to correct some flaw or groove some amendment. You should also allow a little extra time before every round you play to hit a few looseners. Develop this habit and you should find yourself saving a couple of shots at the beginning of each round.

This should not be a full-scale session as practice is more tiring than many people think and could lead to fatigue creeping in at the end of the round. Just hit four or five shots with a variety of clubs, starting with a 9-iron or wedge and building up to the longer clubs. Always finish, though, with a few short pitches and if possible some chips and putts.

Adopting this habit can often lead to ribbing from your fellow members and accusations of trying too hard. Remember though, as you take their money, he who laughs last, laughs longest.

Preparation

As well as practising, there are a few other tips to help you produce your best golf more often. Most of these concern getting to the first tee in the right physical and mental shape to play properly.

First and foremost, allow yourself enough time, so that you don't arrive on the first tee out of breath and flustered. Having built a time to hit warm-up shots into your schedule, be aware of how long this takes, especially picking the balls up afterwards. You should always aim to be hitting a few putts on the putting green five minutes before you tee off.

It was said that Bobby Locke worked at his tempo for the day from the moment he woke up. He tied his shoe laces at the same speed as he swung the club – slowly and methodically. For the amateur, this may be taking matters a bit far, but the chances of hitting a good shot off the first tee are greatly improved if you haven't arrived there in a rush.

Really work at playing the first hole well, as this can set the pattern for the day. Even if you have got to the tee well on time, the opening shots can be a bit stressful, so try not to hit flat out and concentrate on a nice easy rhythm. Even if you are confident with a driver, it can often be beneficial to take a 3-wood just to make sure that the first shot finds the fairway.

Nice as it is to have bacon and eggs with all the trimmings for breakfast, very rarely can your best golf be produced on a full stomch. Tea and toast, plus a few snacks in the bag for halfway round, is a much better recipe.

Likewise, the afternoon round. Half a bottle of red wine, plus a couple of Kummels, may indeed eliminate any anxiety on the first tee, but it will also create fatigue near the end, and that's when the money's won and lost.

As I have mentioned quite often, it is important to have positive thoughts how each shot should be played. You should also have a swing plan for the day and stick to it throughout. It is easy to start off concentrating on a slow takeaway, or keeping the head behind the ball, but all too often the plan flies out the window with the first bad shot. The worst thing you can ever do is try and correct some imagined fault while out on the course. So, stick with the game plan – let your opponent fiddle with his swing when things go wrong.

With a good score in prospect and only a few holes to go, the adrenalin begins to flow. Be aware that this will probably cause you to hit harder without realizing it. Even the top playing professionals are aware of this phenomenon and adjust their club selection accordingly. As the pressure mounts, take one club less and be certain to hit it firmly.

Many is the amateur, particularly the high handicap one, who reaches for an iron club on a short hole, regardless of its length. Whether it's vanity, or worry about seeming inadequate, I do not know, but time and again I have seen a less than competent golfer take the hardest club in the bag – the 2-iron – when he needs his best hit with a driver, or at least a 3-wood, to get there. Also the best shape of shot to a short hole is usually the higher flight and dropping trajectory produced by a 3- or 4-wood.

Whilst on the subject of clubs off the tee, the condition of the course can cause a change of plan. In a dry summer, fairways can become hard and bouncy. The extra distance provided by the driver, so attractive in the winter, can become a positive liability, when there is a lot of run on the ball. This is why you see many professionals using the 1-iron off the tee – length is of far less concern than accuracy. For the amateur in these conditions, a 3-wood will not result in much loss of distance and the wayward tee shot will be less inclined to shoot away into trouble.

Tactics

In any competitive situation, whether it be medal or match play, wasting shots is both irritating to you and reassuring for your opponent. Look back over your recent rounds and see where you dropped shots unnecessarily. Bad shots are inevitable. It is how you react to them and how you try to extricate yourself from the resultant trouble that dictate whether you throw shots away.

If you are hitting the ball reasonably well and have more or less the right handicap, you ought to have sufficient shots in hand to make sure of getting out of whatever trouble you find, without being too worried about the probability of dropping a shot. Most disasters stem from attempting too much with a recovery and hitting the ball into a worse mess as a result. It is strange how, if you accept that a particular bad shot is going to mean a dropped shot and play accordingly, the resultant careful recovery can sometimes lead to a good pitch and putt and a rescued par.

Continuing with the theme of having positive thoughts when playing each shot, every golfer should have a clear idea how he is going to tackle any given hole. To do this, he must be honest with himself as to his own limitations and capabilities as a golfer. Here is a check list of things to consider when planning your play:

1. Which is the best side of the fairway to play the second shot from? The answer to this will usually be dictated by the pin position and will be the opposite side of the fairway to that part of the green where the pin is. Other factors are the position of bunkers guarding the approaches to the green and whether the green slopes from one side or other. Ideally, you should always try to place the tee shot to give yourself a clear shot into the green (not coming in over bunkers), with the ball pitching INTO any appropriate slope. A good example is the 15th hole on the West course at Wentworth, well known to television viewers. A par 4, the hole doglegs

The 15th on Wentworth's West Course, and in the foreground the bunker close to the ideal spot from which to play the second shot

from left to right. The green slopes down from the right-hand side and there is a bunker guarding the front, right-hand corner. As a result, the further you can keep the ball down the left-hand side of the fairway, the easier will be the second shot. It can then be played in without having to flirt with the bunker on the right and the ball will be pitching into the upslope. Incidentally, what makes it a great hole, is the large bunker threatening the drive down the left-hand side, forcing you back the other way.

2. Another consideration is, should you miss a fairway, which is the least damaging side to do it? Also at Wentworth, the 17th is a good example. Out of bounds lurks up the left-hand side and that always means 2 shots dropped. From the other side there is still a fair chance of a par, even from the light rough. At our level of golf though, this hole is usually reachable in 2, so a par feels like a dropped shot.

3. Having found the fairway, or maybe surveying a short hole, it is not always advisable to go for the pin. It may well be cut dangerously close to bunkers or other trouble and require an almost perfect shot even to find the green at that point. Taking Wentworth again, the 2nd hole is a perfect example. When the pin is placed on the right-hand side, the green is only half as deep as the left. There is a cavernous bunker guarding the front at that point and the branches of the oak on the right corner actually overhang the pin there. To go for the pin leaves absolutely no margin for error. Play for the 'fat' of the green and you have three times the size of target, the certainty of a 3, and longish putts have been known to drop. Also, at that early point of the round, it would be wrong to take risks. If it were one of the last three holes and you desperately needed a birdie or two to win, then the plan could well be different.

4. When faced with a dogleg off the tee, it is tempting to shape the drive to match the contours of the hole. Fine if you are a competent golfer or a touring pro, but hazardous for the higher handicap amateur. It is best to select the widest part of the fairway within range and try to hit a straight shot to it. This is particularly true if the angle of the dogleg has a ditch, heavy rough or trees. At best you will be saving yourself a club or two on the second shot whilst risking the possibility of a lost ball. It's just not worth it.

Opposite: *The 17th at Wentworth. Out of bounds on the left and the fairway slanted to throw the ball towards the rough on the right*

5. Finally, on the putting green, approach long putts conscious of which side of the hole you want the ball to finish on, in the likely event of it not going in. Always, and this applies to shots to the green as well, try and leave yourself an uphill putt – so much easier to hole and so much easier to have a positive go at, without risk of a horrid one back.

These thoughts are designed to prevent you chucking shots away in a medal round, or presenting holes to a match play opponent – nothing is more damaging to your confidence or helpful to his. Just think how hard birdies are to come by and what a waste to give them away in handfuls. Adopting the above thoughts and advice won't eliminate them entirely, but if you can cut out the vast majority, your handicap could well come down and the Sunday morning take increase.

Epilogue: The Year After

What to do for an encore

I suppose, in retrospect, 1988 was always going to be a difficult year. For as long as I can remember, life, let alone golf, had been the ongoing struggle for survival. True, things had got better and better and by the start of 1987 I knew that, barring some horrible and permanent loss of form, golf was going to make me a very comfortable living and probably a well-insulated old age.

But I still had my mountains to climb. I wanted to be regarded as one of the best, if not *the* best. There were still the kings of Europe – Seve Ballesteros, Nick Faldo, Bernhard Langer and Sandy Lyle – who were always quoted amongst the top half dozen in the world, and then there were the rest of us on the European Tour.

The early part of 1987 was good, very good by my standards, but still consolidation rather than breaking new ground. I just won more often and made more money than in previous years. After a great run-up to and through the Open Championship, my game went off the boil in August and early September. It wasn't till I saw a recording of some of my play in the European Open on television that I noticed the lower half of my body had become very stiff – the legs too straight. Straight up to the course for a practice, a final round of 65 and I was back on song.

Looking back, that quiet spell may have been a good thing. It's impossible to go on playing your best golf all the time and being in contention week after week takes a tremendous toll on one's reserves. Whilst I had still played a lot of golf, I entered the autumn competitively refreshed and full of enthusiasm for the game, knowing I had sorted out the problem that had caused the poor form of the previous few weeks.

It was the last four months of 1987 that turned a very good year into a fantastic one. The euphoria of being a part of that historic Ryder Cup match carried me through to victory in the World Match Play and from then until the end of the year I would have played anyone anywhere, and fancied myself to win.

Suddenly, I had taken the last few rungs up the ladder of my ambitions in a rush. On my day I was as good as anyone else in the world. The win at Sun City had taken my year's earnings past the £1m mark and I could say for the first time that I was financially secure for the rest of my days. I had joined my heroes at the top of the tree. I had done it.

To succeed in anything, you've got to have targets. I now needed to set myself new ones, though I wasn't aware of it at the time. Looking back, my mistake was to see 1988 as a year of marking time, of consolidation. Maybe a victory or two, perhaps a major title, the belief that these things would come almost as a matter of course, provided I kept my form and health. In reality, I didn't set myself tough enough targets and within a few months I, along with the rest of the world, wondered if perhaps the deeds of 1987 had been just a flash in the pan.

What I hadn't realized was the extraordinary change in my way of life the successes of 1987 would create. Up till then, I had gone where I chose in pursuit of golf tournaments and rested when I felt it necessary. Now, suddenly, there were lucrative opportunities in many parts of the world and, above all, new deals to be done.

With a lot of endeavour I had become very good at golf. My main decisions had been which club to play and what line to hit my putts on. I was suddenly pitched into a world where I was no better than 15 handicap at many of the things expected of a so-called star performer. What to say to the press, how to dress for a television interview, what deals to go for, and what to reject. Having become confident in handling all aspects of my life, I was suddenly a bit at sea in a number of different ways and, looking back, I feel this uncertainty permeated through to my golf game as well.

The press made much of my change of clubs, and certainly it was another change in a period when many things were changing. I do not for one minute regret making the switch. The set I have now is as good, or better, than anything I have ever played with. It was just that changing one more element at a time when so much else was being turned upside down was, I suppose, tempting providence.

That said, the new clubs saga may just have been a blessing in disguise. Even with the old clubs, I would probably have taken time to adjust to the new world I was operating in, and the start of the year would have been just as bad. But they did give me something to blame, or at least justify, my apparent loss of form. At least there was a reason and I didn't go fiddling with my swing, which might have been even more damaging in the long term.

I was also lucky that when I once again got into a position to win, at the PGA at Wentworth, I did win. What pleased me most was how strongly I finished, with Seve breathing down my neck. That, above all else, proved to me that the previous year was no fluke. Thereafter, it was just a case of getting the clubs totally right and that came after a visit to Japan in August. In the end, three victories on the European Tour and 4th place on the money list were perhaps more than I had set out to achieve.

My goals for the next couple of years are now clearly defined. The Sony rankings are the statistical evidence of who is the best golfer in the world and I want to top that. And, of course, that ever-elusive major championship.